Advance Praise for
From the Bench to the Boardroom

"*From the Bench to the Boardroom*, Michael MacDonald shares his journey from his college basketball career at Rutgers to executive positions at Xerox and Medifast. His leadership, work ethic, and persistence, which were on display every step of the way, have made him a valued member of our board at the Jimmy V Foundation."

—**Mike Krzyzewski**, Naismith Hall of Fame coach, Duke University

"Mike MacDonald has been a tremendous influence in my life over the last twenty years. He is first of all a powerful business leader whose style of leadership has been way ahead of its time. Although his credentials speak for themselves, his ability to command respect comes not from an 'up one down one' old-school paternalistic style prevalent all too long in business.

"Instead he creates a team environment that focuses on people and addresses the human side of business. He is a master of understanding the whole person, not just what they can provide in terms of results. He recognizes relationships that are built on empowerment not dependency allow the whole team to become collaborative and develop an ownership mentality. The result fosters total accountability, personal responsibility, and group and organizational dynamics that are essential especially at times like these when responsiveness and agility is essential for success.

"Today, much like the final minutes in a basketball game, we must pivot in days and weeks rather than in months to years. Mike's strong sports background has taught him inherent instincts that I observed on so many occasions that have allowed us to overcome adversity, adapt, and win when the weak would have collapsed.

"In fact, when I met Mike, Optavia was an insignificant three-million-dollar-a-year company and over the last six years under his watch it has grown to almost a billion dollars. This has been a direct result of Mike's willingness to work with all of the stakeholders including my team of leaders and create a joint accountability for our circumstances and our results.

"In fact, during the last six months of uncertainty, fear, and survival mode for most, our organization is thriving and growing rapidly as a result of the organizational health and culture Mike has fostered in our people and our coaches. It's nothing less than miraculous.

"Beyond business, I consider Mike not only a colleague and a mentor but also a close personal friend who has taught me so much and set such an example with his relational skills and his focus on values.

"He is indeed someone to be modeled in his approach to business and life.

"You will find such wisdom within this book that can help in so many ways.

"It can guide you in your approach to business to improve your capabilities and your results. It can help develop you into a more compassionate people-focused leader, much as it has helped me understand how to build an organizational culture that is fit for purpose during these uncertain times.

"Great leaders reinforce the idea that accomplishment in our society comes from great individual acts. We credit individuals for outcomes that require teams and communities to accomplish.

"Mike knows this and together we have helped impact millions of people's lives. That type of leadership guidance and organizational culture has never been needed more."

—**Dr. Wayne Scott Andersen**; Cofounder, Optavia; Author of the *Habits of Health* Transformational System; *New York Times* Bestselling Author; 10th Board Certified Critical Care Physician; Former Director, Surgical Critical Care, Grandview Hospital; Former Chairman, Department of Anesthesiology

"If you have ever been a part of a team, one of the most important reputations you can have is being a good teammate. A good teammate shares the values and ideals of his team. A good teammate shows appreciation for the opportunities he is provided and takes advantage of these opportunities to advance themselves and others. A good teammate makes his other teammates—and overall team—better through their involvement and leadership.

"I never played a sport with Mike MacDonald at Rutgers. Mike and I were never even on campus as student-athletes at the same time. However, I am proud and fortunate to call Mike MacDonald one of my—and Rutgers'—greatest 'teammates.'

"While our paths didn't cross during our respective times 'on the Banks,' I became acquainted with Mike toward the end of my NFL career and post-football life. I quickly learned that, like me, Mike holds a deep reverence and appreciation for his time at Rutgers, as well as for the opportunities that Rutgers has provided him. As a letterwinner on the Rutgers men's basketball teams in the 1970s, Mike took his student-athlete experience and translated these learned lessons to successes in his career.

"Throughout his professional career, Mike's used his successes to help advance his beloved Rutgers. As an involved alumnus, his vocal leadership and commitment to positioning Rutgers as a continued leader in higher education has continued to be invaluable. Like any clutch teammate, Mike's philanthropic efforts in advancing the opportunities for current Rutgers student-athletes have set Rutgers Athletics up for long-term success.

"Mike may have left Rutgers, but Rutgers has never been forgotten by Mike. His time as a Rutgers student-athlete, alumnus, board member, donor, and father/father-in-law of three Rutgers alumni continues to leave an indelible legacy on our alma mater.

"All of this is to say that Mike MacDonald has most certainly solidified himself as a great teammate of Rutgers University. For me, through our professional and personal interactions and relationship, I am proud to call him not only a great teammate, but an even better friend."

—**Marco Battaglia**, Rutgers Football All-American and Cincinnati Bengals Player

"I believe the combination of an excellent education and participation in highly competitive sports programs provides invaluable preparation for life after school is over. The best sources of knowledge about the benefits of such a background are people who have been there. Mike MacDonald fits the bill. And he is particularly well suited to write about his experiences because of an amazing ability to recollect the details of his formative years. A student athlete at Rutgers, he was part of the school's then outstanding basketball team. He went on to use this and similar pre-college experiences to build an exceptional business career. That's part of his story but those of us who know him well would add that he is the epitome of a 'good man.' I have seen him close up with family, friends, and others for years. He is a great husband, dad, and grandfather, kind and generous, enthusiastic, and always on the go. You will enjoy what he has to say."

—**Gene Renna**, Retired Senior Executive, Exxon Mobil

"Mike MacDonald represents the absolute best of Rutgers University and is an inspiration to everyone on campus. From the day I met Mike, he has always made himself available to mentor, guide, and motivate both our student-athletes and our coaching staff. As an alumnus, he has given back generously and led the charge in ensuring that Rutgers continues to be a beacon of higher education.

"I've always admired his ability to juggle the roles of family man, businessman, and leader in the Rutgers community. His path from Rutgers is a shining example for student-athletes of the future. He has succeeded in every aspect of life and continues to give back to the community that molded him.

"To give Mike MacDonald the ultimate compliment a coach can give, simply put, he is a WINNER."

—**Steve Pikiell**, Head Men's Basketball Coach, Rutgers University

FROM *the* BENCH *to the* BOARDROOM

FROM *the* BENCH *to the* BOARDROOM

MY JOURNEY *from*
UNDERDOG ATHLETE
to TURNAROUND CEO

MICHAEL C. MACDONALD
with DICK WEISS

PRESS

A POST HILL PRESS BOOK

From the Bench to the Boardroom:
My Journey from Underdog Athlete to Turnaround CEO
© 2021 by Michael C. MacDonald
All Rights Reserved

ISBN: 978-1-64293-756-5
ISBN (eBook): 978-1-64293-757-2

Cover art by Cody Corcoran
Cover photo by Michael Cassella
Interior design and composition by Greg Johnson, Textbook Perfect

Post Hill Press
New York • Nashville
posthillpress.com

Published in the United States of America
1 2 3 4 5 6 7 8 9 10

Dedication by Michael MacDonald

This book is dedicated with love and appreciation to:

My wife, Jean—you've been a steadfast partner on this incredible journey
and the best mom our kids could ask for.

My children, Ryan, Stacey, and Chris—being your dad has been
the most rewarding "job" and my greatest success.

My grandchildren, Reese, Roree, Ryten, Christian, and Cameron—
being your Pop Pop has been the most fun "job" I've ever had.
It brings me more joy than you will ever know.

My son-in-law, Anthony, and my daughter-in-law, Lauren—
being your father-in-law has been the easiest "job," making the "in-law"
feel unnecessary. I treasure you as I do my own children.

The rest of my family—being a part of this "team"
keeps me humble and grateful.

Dedication by Dick Weiss

I want to dedicate this book to Patrick Plunkett
for his invaluable help framing this book.

He is a reformed coach who is currently involved
in college development but would have been a great sports columnist
if he had chosen to go into that profession.

He was my go-to guy when I worked for the New York *Daily News*
and was looking for prospective in college basketball.

Like Mike, his priority is now his family.

Contents

Foreword

By Dick Vitale

In 1971, when I arrived on the campus of Rutgers University as a member of the basketball coaching staff, I had my first opportunity to meet Michael MacDonald. Our head coach, Dick Lloyd, during the evaluation process described Michael as a sharpshooter who was from Philadelphia, the City of Brotherly Love. In my first meeting with Michael, I knew immediately that this young guy had special qualities that would separate him from the rest. When I shook his hand, I was immediately impressed by how he looked you straight in the eye and spoke with a great deal of confidence. I walked away and said to myself that this young guy was going to make it in the biggest game of all, "the game of life."

Michael, in his second year at Rutgers, was hoping to gain some major minutes utilizing a great jump shot that he possessed, but unfortunately for him, we had recruited one of the premier classes in the nation. The group we were fortunate to bring to the Rutgers campus will go down in Rutgers history as one of the greatest classes ever assembled. The "Diaper Dandies" were led by the dynamic duo of Phil Sellers and Mike Dabney, who went on to superstardom and led Rutgers to the Final Four in 1976. Also joining Rutgers in the battle for the 1976 NCAA Championship were Indiana, Michigan, and UCLA. The title ultimately was won by Bob Knight and the Hoosiers, who remain the last team to finish with a perfect record. The point that I am making here is that, due to our recruiting success, it cost Michael a chance to get the kind of playing time that he was hoping for. Little did I know at that time that the qualities that I witnessed in Michael would later play a role in his becoming a giant in the corporate world. I was so impressed by how he was so dedicated to his teammates, and his loyalty was off the charts. Michael was always about the *team*: "T" for "togetherness," "E" for "effort," "A" for "attitude," and "M" for "mental toughness"! I knew immediately that Michael MacDonald would be headed for success big-time once he finished his academic and athletic career in a Rutgers uniform. How did he become such a giant in the business world? Very simply, through an incredible work ethic, commitment, and a positive attitude that became infectious with everyone who crossed his path. Michael epitomizes the saying "The only place you can find success ahead of work is in the dictionary."

Michael MacDonald is one of the most well-liked and respected people I have ever known. He started his career after college pursuing a graduate degree when he joined head coach Jim Valvano (a former Rutgers basketball player) as a graduate assistant at Iona College. He loved coaching but finally decided to make the transition to the business world. He joined Xerox Corporation, where he started on the bottom and worked his way up the ladder, ultimately becoming the president of the largest division of a major corporation. His is an amazing story, as he went from sitting on the bench as a collegiate athlete to sitting in a boardroom as a prime-time executive because of energy and enthusiasm, but most of all because of his incredible work ethic. Another great quality that Michael possesses is that he always treats people like he wants to be treated. I had saw him in action firsthand when I was the featured motivational speaker at a Xerox convention. I was so impressed by the respect he received from everyone in the crowd. That respect came due to his caring personality in that he treated everyone equally no matter what their stature was.

Talk about being more than just a business giant; he made himself available for various charities, and the one that has meant so much to him has been the V Foundation for Cancer Research. It is named after his good friend the late Jim Valvano. Michael is a highly respected member of the board of directors of the V Foundation, of which I am also a proud member. Michael has been a major contributor to the V Foundation in many ways. He has been vital as a donor financially, but more important has done an amazing job in raising awareness of what the V Foundation is all about. He is also very proud to have served on the board of trustees at Rutgers University. He has shared with me on many occasions that he feels that the many good fortunes that have happened in him in his life have come because of the many learning experiences he had as a student athlete at Rutgers.

This book will provide you with the opportunity to analyze and evaluate the many ideas and concepts that Michael MacDonald used to climb the ladder of success. Competing in the corporate world can be very intense and competitive, and using this book as a tool can provide you with that winning edge! If I were on TV right now, I would simply say, "Michael, you are awesome, baby, with a capital 'A'! You are a genuine PTPer [prime-time performer]. You are the 'Three S' man: super, scintillating, sensational in the biggest game of all, the game of life!"

CHAPTER 1

Humble Beginnings

Even though I was only thirty minutes away from the Main Line mansions, I was a world away growing up in Upper Darby, a working-class suburban community on the outskirts of Philadelphia.

Our neighborhood was filled with row houses, turn-of-the-century single homes, and small businesses and bars on the main thoroughfare, West Chester Pike. This was a major highway that served the 69th Street Terminal, the last stop for city subways; the terminal connected to buses, trolleys, and regional rail lines into Delaware County.

It was the first streetcar suburb and was filled with families who were in search of the American Dream. It was also a world away from the ever-changing neighborhoods in the city and a haven from the racial tensions and the blockbusting going on there. Upper Darby was a line of demarcation. There used to be two department stores—Gimbels and Lit Brothers—in the shopping district up the hill from the Tower Theater, Philly's version of the Fillmore in New York City. The Tower Theater brought some of the biggest names in music to its stage, like Paul Simon, Neil Young, David Bowie, U2, the Grateful Dead, Bob Marley, the Rolling Stones and Bob Dylan.

It was a place that forged my character. Blue-collar families shared their values, believed in education, and made Sunday mass and Eagles football a priority. It was a place where I learned about myself. It was my little universe, and those of us who lived there believed we could control our destiny through hard work, hustle, and being competitive enough to realize that if we wanted to be relevant, we had to master something.

My parents grew up there and attended Upper Darby High School, but neither graduated. My father, Bradley, worked sixteen hours a day driving a truck for Sealtest Dairy and then drove a taxi for the Yellow Cab Company. My mother, Florence, used to perform with a touring dance troupe known as the Roxyettes, a forerunner to the Radio City Rockettes in New York City. They performed at all the local theaters, including the Mastbaum Theatre. With five thousand seats, the Mastbaum was the largest and most lavish movie palace ever built in Philadelphia, and used to host stage shows as well. My mother also was part of a three-person dance troupe in vaudeville.

My parents got married in the Great Depression, prior to World War II, and my father received a hardship deferment from the service because he was supporting a family and supporting his mother. When I was growing up, my mom worked part-time as a clerk for State Farm Insurance, but she basically was a stay-at-home mom.

We had a big family. I was the sixth of seven children, and there are only three of us left. My oldest sister, Margaret, is eighty-three. I am sixty-seven. My younger brother, Bobby, is sixty-four. I had three other sisters—Florence, Mary, and Marilyn—and a big brother, Brad.

In the 1950s, it seemed like everybody in our neighborhood had lots of kids and no money. When I was growing up, my family never owned a home. We used to rent, then move if the owner wanted the house back. I lived in five different houses and apartments as a kid. I got used to moving. We didn't have much furniture. When I was six, we moved into a five-bedroom home on Park Avenue near West Chester Pike, next to the firehouse across the street from Saint Laurence Parish's grade school. I will never forget the fire sirens going off all the time when I was a kid, trying to go to sleep.

My family always seemed to be expanding. We had eleven people if you count my grandmother and my aunt who were living with us. When Margaret got married, she and her husband moved to Ohio, then her husband received a job transfer and they moved back in with us, with their kids. At one time, we had fourteen people living in our house. We even had a boarder—a cab driver my father knew.

We would have huge family meals every weekend. They were like family reunions. My mother's brothers—who were in the elevator business—and sisters and my father's two brothers would all come over. We would have twenty to twenty-five people at the tables with all kinds of grandchildren running around. My uncles would contribute to the food, and my mother would cook. We had typical meals: ham and cabbage or lamb one night, then leftovers the next.

As my sisters got married and the family got smaller, we moved into an apartment over Sharkey's clothing store on West Chester Pike. When Bobby and I were the only children left, we lived in an apartment over a barber shop, then a small two-bedroom house on Park Avenue off State Road near a Wawa food market.

Holidays were always an adventure. Close to Christmas, my mother would go to Ritter Finance and borrow money to buy Christmas presents for everybody. We didn't get many presents because there were so many kids and grandchildren. The Ritter Finance guy would come after the holidays to collect, and my mother would tell us, "Don't answer the door." We would lie low until he left, and she would eventually pay the bill off.

My parents were Scottish and English. My mother converted to Catholicism; she understood we needed to be part of a bigger community. My father converted after my brother Brad joined the seminary. My mother was the type of person who went to church on special occasions, but every Sunday she pushed us all out the door to go to Mass at Saint Laurence and then she'd stay home. I was an altar boy for a while and sang in the choir at church. All the kids I knew in my neighborhood went to Saint Laurence. Back then, there were large classrooms with sixty children seated two to a desk, and everybody was taught by the nuns from the Immaculate Heart of Mary order. They were tough. They would smack us with a ruler if we got out of hand. I can still remember where I was in 1963 the day John F. Kennedy, the first Catholic president, died. The nuns called us into a classroom, told us the tragic news, then sent us home to pray.

Funny story. When I was working as an altar boy in second grade, Father Langan at Saint Laurence gave me the six a.m. masses three weeks in a row in January, and it was freezing cold that year. I'd have to get up at five in the morning, and I was falling asleep in class. I decided, the heck with that. I left that job. Years later, after college, I was interviewing for a job at Xerox and I was introduced to Howard Langan, the branch manager in Princeton, New Jersey. I walked in and he said to me, "Mike, where are you from?"

I told him I was from Upper Darby.

And he said, "Do you know my brother, Father Langan?"

And I said, "Well, don't call him for a reference." I told him about quitting as an altar boy.

He hired me, called his brother, and said, "Hey, Father, I saved one of your lost souls."

I learned at a young age that your personal values are your number-one priority in your life—how you treat people: your family, your friends, your elders. I always had tremendous respect for my father and mother and a strong relationship with my brothers and sisters. Today, I still speak with Margaret and Bob three or four times a week.

Margaret had some talent as an artist and attended Pennsylvania Academy of the Fine Arts, but she didn't have the money to finish. She eventually got married and became a successful Realtor. She raised six children on her own after her husband left. She still lives in the area, out by Villanova University.

Bob was an Army guy who worked as a prison guard at Fort Sill in Oklahoma. He spent his whole life in law enforcement. He went to Indiana University of Pennsylvania in Punxsutawney, but dropped out of college after six months, then enlisted in the military. When he got out of the Army, he went back to school and graduated from Texas A&M University-Corpus Christi and got into law enforcement in Texas. He spent twenty-five years with the Corpus Christi police department, then was a chief of police in two Texas towns, Jasper and Uvalde, before he retired in Houston.

For a long time, we didn't own a car. Then my uncle Harvey gave my parents a white Plymouth Valiant. He attended the University of Delaware, where he played football and baseball, and then played briefly for the 1928 Phillies. He did not last long in the majors. He had only fifteen to twenty at-bats in his only year in the big leagues, and wound up managing Llanerch Country Club in nearby Havertown and a hotel in Lansdale. My uncle Charlie played basketball for Temple University. He was a civil engineer who helped design the Pennsylvania Turnpike. He was also the guy who taught me how to play golf on the public courses a couple of miles away from my home. Both of my uncles were college graduates who had attended Winona Military Academy in Delaware. Unfortunately, my father never had those opportunities.

His father, Charles Everett MacDonald, was a major and a famous chief surgeon in the Army on the Argonne front in World War I. He is buried in Arlington Cemetery along with my two uncles, who both served in World War I. He married my grandmother and they had four children, Charles, Brad, Harvey, and Mary. But the marriage didn't last.

After the divorce, my grandfather Charles moved to Washington, D.C., got remarried, had other children, and never kept in touch. My father was left to take care of his mother, so he never got a chance to go to college. He worked hard, and after he was done for the day, his big form of relaxation would be to hit the bars on West Chester Pike. I can still remember my mother saying to me, "Go get Bradley."

I'd run up to the bar and get my dad, who would be sitting at the bar with a beer in his hand. Occasionally, he'd let me sit on a bar stool and nurse a Coke. My father was never an athlete, but he loved sports and the local teams—the Phillies, the Eagles, and the 76ers. He always wore a Phillies cap to work. I remember he took me to two professional sporting events. I was at Convention Hall in West Philly for game five of the 1967 NBA finals between the 76ers and the San Francisco Warriors. Wilt Chamberlain was my favorite athlete. But that night, Rick Barry went off for forty points and the Warriors won, 117–109. The Sixers wound up winning the title the next game in San Francisco. Championships were few and far between for long-suffering Philly fans. We went to see the Eagles play the Chicago Bears in an NFL game at Franklin Field on the campus of the University of Pennsylvania. Gale Sayers scored four touchdowns for the Bears, and Dick Butkus had eighteen tackles.

It seemed like my dad was always working. So, my mom handled the discipline at home. If she said to do something, we were going to do it. One time, I made the mistake of giving my mother a hard time and I told her I was going to run away. I was sitting outside our house and my mother rolled out my basketball and said, "Well, I hope you can eat this."

My parents were not overly affectionate, but we knew they loved us. If we were playing in a game, we knew my mom and dad would be there. My mom drove me back and forth to high school as well.

When I was in college, my sister Marilyn died during open heart surgery at age thirty-three. She had a six-month-old baby, Melissa, whom our family raised as their own. Marilyn had lived at home the longest and had always taken the family on road trips. I will always treasure those memories. She instilled a passion for history and travel that has stayed with me.

There were good times and difficult times when I was growing up, but overall, Upper Darby was a wonderful place to grow up. Most of the families were Irish, Italian, or German, all trying to improve their lives. Everybody knew one another and everybody watched out for one another. We used to have parades on the Fourth of July; we'd decorate our bikes for them, then play a baseball game in the afternoon. We all cared about each other, but at the same time none of us wanted to be the last kid picked in any game.

There were a couple of motorcycle gangs to avoid, but other than that, there was not much crime in Upper Darby. No one had anything worth stealing. The only thing people valued was a picture of Kennedy in the hallway.

I was an average student at Saint Laurence through sixth grade, then I made the honor roll my last two years in grade school. My love of learning was forged by the Chip Hilton and Hardy Boys books I read. Chip Hilton is a fictional high school three-sport star who is often placed in a position of persuading his less-than-perfect teammates to play his way and share his values—with winning championships as a result. The Chip Hilton books, written by Hall of Fame basketball coach Clair Bee, have sold more than two million copies to date. They were always about a kid who worked hard, and they always had a happy ending. I'd sit and read on summer days when it was too hot to go out.

I wasn't a guy with eight hundred friends. I made three good friends when I was younger. Nick Cangi grew up over by the observatory playground. I met him and Dave Gladfelter, who lived a couple blocks away, when we were in first grade. Mike Rush was a year behind us in school; he had a younger brother named Steve who used to hang out with us as well.

Mike's dad worked with the IRS, and Nick's father was a bricklayer. Dave's father was a chemist and taught me how to play chess. He wasn't into sports, but his kids all played musical instruments. I never played music. My brother played the accordion. He was so bad, he used to drive me nuts. Mike played basketball at Monsignor Bonner High School, a large Catholic school run by Augustinian priests, and wound up graduating and getting an advanced degree from Drexel University before becoming the head of the tax division at IKON Office Solutions. Nicky went to Delaware County Community College and made the basketball team, but he left after a semester to become a conductor on the local freight trains. Nicky is retired now, and the family lives in nearby Springfield. Dave attended Philadelphia Textile and does construction repairs in New Jersey. Steve played basketball at Bonner and Textile and was hired by Xerox in sales, then went into selling prosthetics.

We would all take the subway to watch the local college teams play at the Palestra or the 76ers play at the Spectrum. "We didn't have much interest in girls when we were young," Nick recalls today. "We were happy as long as we had a basketball." We all liked sports and played whatever was in season. We even tried bowling. But basketball was the sport of choice in our neighborhood.

They were all nice kids and are still my best friends today, sixty years later. When I worked for Xerox, I spent fifteen years in Rochester, New York, but anytime I was in the area, we would all get together for dinner.

"I can still remember Mike coming over to our house," Nick recalls. "My mom would just point him in the direction of the cookie jar. We were both so skinny, we could have eaten boxes of cookies and it wouldn't have mattered."

The first organized sports teams I played on were through the Highland Park Kirklyn Athletic Association. The first sport I played was fast-pitch softball; I was six years old and played second base. I didn't start playing basketball until sixth grade. I was skinny and really didn't have a lot of confidence growing up. But with four sisters, I needed to get out of the house just to get some peace. So my friends and I would go up to the basketball courts in the observatory playground. When it snowed, we would shovel the courts to play.

As you can imagine, it didn't take long to wear my sneakers out. I asked my mother if I could get a new pair of Converse shoes. Brad and I both wore size eleven, so he went into the closet and threw me a pair of his old black low-top Chuck Taylors, and told me to pull them on and wear them until she could afford to buy me new ones. One thing about old sneakers: They hurt. They didn't fit right. My brother was much bigger than me. But that's the way life was back then. Eventually, I got a pair of black high-tops.

They didn't help my game that much. I made our Catholic Youth Organization (CYO) team, but I didn't play much as a sixth and seventh grader.

I was slow to develop. I would get easily pushed around on the court. I weighed maybe a hundred pounds in eighth grade. Danny Boudwin was six foot two and was the star of our eighth-grade team, weighing forty to fifty pounds more than me.

Occasionally, I'd bring Brad with me to the courts and he'd beat the hell out of me. Brad was six years older than me, and he was a big guy.

Brad was a great role model. He was a good baseball and basketball player, but not good enough to make the team at Bonner. He loved sports and used to take me to watch Bonner play in the Philadelphia Catholic League. After high school, he joined the Augustinian seminary, got his grades up, then enrolled at Villanova, an Augustinian university, in the Philadelphia suburbs. He got his degree, then joined the Marines on the advice of Father John Melton, who was the guidance counselor at Bonner and had been a Marine Corps chaplain. He rose to the rank of colonel during a twenty-seven-year military career in the Vietnam and Gulf War eras.

Like most brothers, we occasionally had our disagreements.

One time he hit me with an elbow to the head during a pickup game at the observatory and gave me a bloody nose. I was bleeding down my face. I went home and complained to my mother.

She said to me, "Don't take that stuff. Hit him back."

"But mom," I said. "He is sixty pounds bigger than me."

Her attitude was, "Get out there. Get back to that court and go back at him again. And never back down." From that point on, I always stood up for myself.

There was plenty of competition at the observatory. There were guys like Danny, John McGregor, and John Cappelletti, who played for Bonner; Bobby Gohl, who played for Upper Darby and earned a scholarship to Villanova; and Jimmy Forte, who played for Saint Joseph's Prep and Textile. I'd try to get there early just to get into a game, and there would be six groups of five, waiting to play the winners. "You would always try to get on a team with Cappelletti, because you knew you would win because he was so competitive," Nick says. "If you lost that first game, you may as well go some other place to play."

I could always shoot, so that was a plus when they were picking teams.

I was fortunate. I had two people—Howard Cusick and Bob Daly—who coached our CYO eighth-grade team at Saint Laurence and had a big impact on my life. Howard knew basketball. He went to Saint Joseph's College when Jack Ramsay coached there. He was tall, about six foot five, and he was still playing pickup basketball long after college. Bob was involved in athletics in the Highland Park recreation leagues.

At Saint Laurence, we always had good CYO teams. I learned a ton from those guys. Howard would drive us over to Memorial Hall in

Fairmount Park to play against some really good young black kids. We played against Tommy Hooks of West Philly and Joe Bryant of Bartram, guys who would eventually become high school and college stars.

When I was in grade school, the biggest sports star in our parish was John Cappelletti, as mentioned above. He was a year older than me. John went on to become a star in football, basketball, and baseball at Bonner. He even threw the javelin for the track team and won the Catholic League championship as a senior.

He was a natural, and when Joe Paterno came to his house to recruit him for Penn State, our whole neighborhood was abuzz. John had a great career at Penn State. Every time he played for the Nittany Lions, I'd try to watch his games on TV. When he was a senior, he won the Heisman Trophy, the most prestigious award in college football, after rushing for 1,522 yards despite absorbing a tremendous amount of pounding. After each game, he would sit in the training room with ice packs all over his body. It usually took multiple defenders to bring him down. When we were younger, we used to play tackle without pads at the golf course near school. If he hit you, you'd be sore for a week.

John was one of four children in his family. The youngest, Joey, was diagnosed with leukemia at the age of three and was one of the first cancer patients to undergo chemotherapy. He sadly passed away at the age of fourteen in 1976. I can still remember John's acceptance speech for the Heisman Trophy. He held back tears as he named Joey as his main source of inspiration because of his bravery and courage while battling the disease. He said that whenever he had temporary feelings of self-pity, he would think about his brother battling leukemia.

"I was healthy," he said. "Who was I to complain about anything? Maybe that was the difference for me, or for the team. Maybe that was the difference between winning and losing the Heisman race."

John dedicated his Heisman Trophy to Joey. He brought Vice President Gerald Ford, Cardinal Fulton J. Sheen, Penn State coach Joe Paterno, and the other 1,700 people in attendance at the Heisman dinner in New York City to tears. He composed his speech just a few hours before the dinner. "If I can dedicate this trophy to him tonight and give him a couple years of happiness, this is worth everything," John said. "I think a lot of people think that I go through a lot on Saturdays, as most athletes do. You get your bumps and bruises, and it's a terrific battle out there on the field. Only for me, it's only on Saturdays and it's only on the field. For Joseph, it's all year round, and it's a battle that is unending for him. He puts up with much more than I'll ever put up with, and I think this trophy is more his than mine, because he has been a great inspiration to me."

One thing about John: He was always humble. A TV movie about John's life and career was eventually made, called *Something for Joey*. It was one of two movies they made about our neighborhood. The other was *Silver Linings Playbook*, starring Bradley Cooper, Jennifer Lawrence, and Robert De Niro. I still remember Upper Darby getting a shout-out in 2017 when Tina Fey, the comedic TV and movie star from my hometown who got her start on *Saturday Night Live*, brought a pizza from one of her favorite local restaurants, Pica's, to *The Late Show* when she did a guest appearance. Pica's still has a plaque in the lobby commemorating the occasion.

Looking back, I know that Upper Darby taught me the value of family—the good, the bad, and the ugly. Nothing is ever perfect in a family. But family is important. Your friends are important. Loyalty, trust, character, ethics—I learned those things early in life. I learned how important education was. My parents didn't graduate high school, but they pushed me and the rest of us to get what they didn't have. In a big family, you're going to have a lot of happiness and a lot of tragedy. The sooner you learn to enjoy family and friends, the better.

CHAPTER 2

Making the Most of Your Opportunities

In 1967, I followed in my brother Brad's footsteps and enrolled at Monsignor Bonner High School. It was run by Augustinian priests, as I mentioned, who also ran nearby Villanova University, and it was located on the top of a hill overlooking the trolley tracks on Garrett Road that led to 69th Street, about two miles from my house. It was next door to Archbishop Prendergast High School for girls. The Archdiocese picked up the two-hundred-dollar annual tuition.

This was the standard course for any student from a local Catholic elementary school.

Bonner was a good fit for me. There were a lot of priests there who were true to their vocation. They gave us a religious and academic foundation and prepared us for college. Some of them even played pickup basketball with us after school in the gym.

Bonner was the largest school in the western suburbs, with an enrollment of 2,400 boys. I went out for the freshman basketball team. It seems like every freshman tried out that day. I never saw so many kids. I got cut right away. To be honest with you, I don't think I should have made the team. I wasn't one of the best fifteen players in my class.

I used to go watch the varsity games, and I got to watch seniors Bob Sabol, Joe Cafferky, and Eddie Hastings—three Division I prospects who went on to play at Saint Joseph's, North Carolina State and Villanova— play. Having seats on those bleachers was like being courtside at Madison Square Garden. Thank goodness there were no scalpers. I couldn't have afforded to get in. But then, just as today, I wanted to be more than a spectator.

I filled the void by playing for our parish CYO team with guys from my neighborhood like John Cappelletti and John McGregor. Although no one was good enough to merit one of those prized Friar jerseys, we were still good. We won the city championship, then beat the best teams in our age group from Maryland through New York to win the Middle Atlantic championship in Towson, Maryland. I was still coming into my own. I was a good shooter, but I wasn't particularly quick, and I was still learning how to be a good rebounder. I came off the bench, and I learned what it was like to play for a championship team. It enforced the value of hard work, and I continued to be hooked on winning. It was something that became ingrained in me, whether I was wearing a necktie or high-tops.

My sophomore year, I went out for the Bonner team again. I felt I was better than some of the guys who made junior varsity. But I didn't have a good tryout. I was nervous and had trouble relaxing. This was one time I didn't make the most of my opportunities. As in any business, if the decision makers don't know who you are and you miss a couple of opportunities, your dreams can get crushed quickly. The silver lining was that a lot of my buddies got cut, too. At least I had someone to walk home from school with. As it became evident later in business, there are only so many seats in the boardroom.

After being cut twice from the team, I was determined to find my name posted outside the lunchroom one way or another.

I became focused on being more than a face in the crowd. This skill could serve me well in basketball tryouts as well as in business interviews. I played for our CYO team again, and I also built up my confidence by playing with Nick Cangi on a team in the Highland Park rec league. I thought Nick had a built-in advantage because he was coached by his father.

It was funny. When I used to come home in high school, my sister Marilyn was still living there. She would work in a doctor's office from eight in the morning until one thirty in the afternoon, then come home and watch the soap operas, have dinner, and then go back to run the night shift. I'd get home at two p.m., and she would always tell me to go out and practice. "You only have two more years at Bonner," she would say. "If you want to make the team, get over to the observatory and work out."

I think she wanted me out of the house so it wouldn't interfere with her watching *General Hospital*.

My junior year, I bulked up to 150 pounds. But I needed to find some way to distinguish myself before tryouts began. And I found the perfect way to make a splash. As luck would have it, I played in an intramural game before tryouts and scored sixty points. I shot the ball unbelievably well that day, and Father Gallimore, one of the priests, went to the Bonner coaches and told them about me. It probably didn't hurt that John Cappelletti also put in a good word for me.

Making Bonner's basketball team was the single biggest achievement of my teenage life. It was the completion of a challenge. I was one of three juniors who made the junior varsity team in 1969, and I was determined not to let this chance slip through my fingers.

"Mike played with us at observatory and Drexel Hill," says Eddie Stefanski, our point guard, of me. He was a year younger and played with me for two years. "You could tell he was a good player, but it was so hard to make the team, because there were eight hundred kids in a class," Eddie says. "There were kids who got regularly got cut from Bonner who still earned scholarships in the fabled Big 5."

It was a unique thing how good the players were in this one area. When I went to Bonner, the freshman coach was Mike Nash, who had played a couple of years at Saint Joe's. He had gone to the same grade school as me, Saint Bernadette's, and knew my older brothers, and I was coming off an eighth-grade season when Saint Bernadette's had gone to the CYO city championship game, so I had a little bit of a reputation coming into tryouts. But I was still worried that if I missed a layup in tryouts, I would get cut, because there was so many kids in the gym.

"I give Mike all the credit in the world. He put a lot of time in. He could always shoot it, got better, worked on quickness. He turned himself into a legit college prospect," Ed Stefanski recalls of my efforts.

Bonner was a traditional basketball power back then, before its enrollment began to dip and coaches began recruiting players from all over the city because parish boundaries were eliminated. When I entered the program, we had twelve players—if you combined JV and varsity—who went on to earn Division I scholarships. Three of them—Jimmy Haggerty, Joe DiCocco, and John Cappelletti—made the All-Catholic team in the Philadelphia Catholic League and the varsity was 24–6. My friends and I used to scrimmage against those three all the time. It gave me a chance to show I was a good offensive player and, in the right circumstances with the right people, I could be successful.

I was one of the top scorers on a good JV team, and I got to suit up for the games, even though I wouldn't be playing during the Philadelphia Catholic League playoffs. Having lost to North Catholic in the semifinals at the Palestra when Cappelletti was injured, we received an invitation to the Alhambra Catholic Invitational Tournament, which featured the best Catholic high schools on the East Coast. In that we defeated Cardinal Dougherty High School, which had beaten North Catholic to win the league championship, in the semifinals. Then we defeated Morgan Wootten's fabled DeMatha Catholic, just outside Washington, D.C., to win the championship when Cappelletti shut down Adrian Dantley, a future All-American at Notre Dame who went on to play in the NBA and was eventually inducted into the Naismith Memorial Basketball Hall of Fame.

When I came home from Alhambra, no one was sure what was going to happen with Bonner's then head coach, Paul Gallagher, when he decided to become an assistant on Paul Westhead's staff at La Salle and devote more time to his real estate career. Bonner hired Dick Bernhart, the quintessential basketball lifer who had been an assistant coach at Swarthmore High for nine years before he joined the Bonner staff in 1970, then moved up.

Dick probably was not as good a basketball coach as Paul Gallagher. But he has the best record of anyone who coached at Bonner. He was an only child who lived with his mom and dad until they passed away, but the players at Bonner were like his second family, whether they were Ed Stefanski, who became a general manager (GM) in the NBA; Harry Peretta, who won six hundred games in his forty-four years as the women's basketball coach at Villanova; Wally Rutecki, who went to Harvard University and became an accomplished Division I basketball official; or six-foot-eight Rodney Blake, who became an All–Big 5 top player at Saint Joseph's.

Dick coached for six years but stayed at the school for thirty, working as the athletic director and dean of men before retiring to Ocean City, New Jersey, in 1998, where he raised boxer dogs and earned a little extra money with an early-morning paper route.

When he turned seventy-five in 2012, a bunch of us got together just before Christmas and held a fundraiser for him at JD McGillicuddy's in Havertown, owned by Thomas Thornton, friend of my brother, Brad. A hundred of his former players showed up. It was a chance for us to say goodbye.

Two days later, after he had driven back to Maryland, he died, and we held a memorial service for him at the school.

I will always remember Dick fondly.

He went out of his way to prepare me to play college basketball. My parents didn't understand anything about college basketball or recruiting. But they always told me to listen to my coaches. Dick used to take me over to the Carriage House, a delicatessen near my house, after practice and buy me two or three milkshakes so I could gain weight, and I put on twenty-five pounds. He got me enrolled in college board classes so I could score over 1,000 on the SAT. And he used to take me over to Swarthmore High School, and I would play one-on-one against Geoff Petrie, a good friend of Dick's who was a big star at Princeton University and was getting ready to enter the NBA as a rookie after being the first-round pick for the Portland

Trail Blazers. He would teach me jab step moves, jab and go, rocker steps, different steps to get my shot off. Geoff was six foot five. He was two and a half inches taller than me. We could play three or four games one-on-one to twenty-one points. He would beat my butt on a regular basis. But one time I beat him. I was thrilled.

The summer before my senior year, I had grown to six foot three and weighed 170 pounds, and Dick asked if I would be interested in attending Pocono Invitational camp at Echo Lake near East Stroudsburg, Pennsylvania, where he worked as a director for the two owners, Temple University's Naismith Hall of Fame coach Harry Litwack and Bill Foster, who was a successful coach at Rutgers University at the time. Bill and Harry met when Bill was at Abington High School and one of his daughters was in Bill's typing class. The two became good friends and business partners, and created a highly successful outdoor summer basketball camp in the mountains for over twenty-five years. It attracted some of the best players on the East Coast and brought in the best coaches in the country—like John Wooden, Bob Knight, and Adolph Rupp—to lecture to the campers.

I was interested, but my parents did not have the money to send me. So, Dick worked out a deal in which I would pay my way by working at the snack bar and serving meals to the campers for a month.

I also worked a week at a football camp there, which was run by Rutgers coach Frank Burns.

One day, I working at the snack bar at the basketball camp and these two huge guys walked in: Richard Wood and Gil Chapman. They were both from Thomas Jefferson High in Elizabeth, New Jersey. Chapman was a tailback/wide receiver who was named Player of the Year by *Parade* and was considered the number-one prospect in the country in 1971; he went on to play four years at the University of Michigan. Rutgers was recruiting both, but so was everyone else in the country. Wood became a three-time All-American linebacker at the University of Southern California.

I rode the bench for a high school three hundred miles away. I may as well have been in the layup line with six hundred kids. I was a ninth grader all over again.

It was great getting to know Bill and Harry. They were both highly principled, ethical people who were trained teachers and great coaches.

My room was located within earshot of the porch, and those guys would sit outside on the porch at night, and I would get a chance to sit and listen to them talk basketball. For me, their conversations were better than listening to a Phillies broadcast. Harry would be smoking his cigars. He wasn't very talkative, but when he did say something it was usually important. All the other coaches respected him. Bill always called him "The Chief" because of the friendly manner in which he greeted people. According to Harry's wife, Estelle, when Harry used to drive a car, if he needed directions and saw a pedestrian walking by, he would say, "Say Chief." It was an expression he used so often when he needed information that people soon began calling him that.

Bill was born in Ridley Park, but grew up in Norwood, Pennsylvania, near Philly. He graduated from Elizabethtown College in 1954 after serving in the Air Force. He became a successful local high school coach at Abington before making the successful transition to college coaching. He started out at Bloomsburg State College before moving on to Rutgers in 1963 and taking his star Dick Lloyd, who coincidentally was from my neighborhood and played at a different playground, with him as his assistant.

His biggest coup was signing Bob Lloyd, Dick Lloyd's little brother, a six-foot-one guard from Upper Darby High School, the public high school that, ironically, Bonner never played. When Bill first approached Bob and showed him a brochure of the school, Bob's first reaction was, "I'm sorry coach, but I'm not interested in a junior college."

Bob was being recruited by all the giants in 1963, including recent NCAA tournament champions Ohio State University and University of Cincinnati. Bill won the recruiting war when Bob chose to stay close to home and sign with Rutgers over Villanova and Davidson College in 1963.

Four years later, he and point guard Jim Valvano put Rutgers on the map when Rutgers made its first postseason appearance ever in 1967 and finished third in the National Invitation Tournament (NIT), ushering in the golden era of Rutgers basketball, which lasted almost two decades.

Bob Lloyd was arguably the best shooter ever to come out of Delaware County. He still holds the record for career scoring average, 26.5 points, and as a senior he led the NCAA Division I in field goal percentage, shooting 92.1 percent and making 225 of 277 attempts. He was the first Rutgers player to have his uniform retired.

"Before we knew the term 'pure shooter,' he was a pure shooter who could do a lot of other things, except play defense," Dick Lloyd recalls. "And you can tell him I said that."

Bob learned how on shoot in his driveway on a backboard pinned to his house. The driveway sloped downward into a basement garage, so the rim height varied depending on where the player stood. "When you shot free throws, you'd be on the same level as the rim," Dick says.

Bob spent countless hours shooting the ball in his backyard, figuring it was the only way he was going to be successful in college. When he was at Rutgers, he would try to make fifty or a hundred free throws in a row before he left practice every day.

But his specialty was his long-range jump shot. Two decades before college basketball instituted the three-point shot in 1966, Bob estimates that he took 60 percent of his shots beyond the arc.

"I didn't even know what a layup was," he says.

As a first-year varsity player in 1965, he put up fifty-one points against Delaware. In 1967, he put up forty-two against Utah State University and forty-four against Marshall University to lead Rutgers to the semifinals. He once made sixty straight free throws.

Harry was older than Bill, one of the true gentlemen in the game. He was born in Galicia, Austria, in 1907 and was raised in a home in Philadelphia where only Yiddish was spoken, and his father, a shoe-maker, never understood basketball. But the game was a huge attraction to immigrant youngsters. "When I was a kid, every phone pole had a peach basket on it," Harry says. "And every Jewish boy played basket-ball." He was a star at Southern High School and a two-time cocaptain at Temple University. He graduated in 1930, then played professionally for six years for Eddie Gottlieb's powerful all-Jewish Philadelphia Sphas. While with the Sphas, Harry served as freshman coach and assistant varsity coach at his alma mater, Temple University. He developed a box-and-one defense in 1937–1938 that held Stanford University's All-America Hank Luisetti, who popularized the jump shot, to eleven points during Temple's 35–31 victory. That same season, the Temple Owls defeated University of Colorado and future Supreme Court judge Byron "Whizzer" White in the first NIT championship game.

Harry served as an assistant to Gottlieb when he was the owner-coach of the Philadelphia Warriors in the early years of the NBA, before being named Temple's head coach in 1952. He coached Temple to a pair of NCAA Final Fours in 1956 and 1958 with a backcourt of consensus All-American future Naismith Hall of Famer Guy Rodgers and Hal Lear, who was selected the tournament's MVP over Bill Russell when he scored forty-eight points in a third-place victory over the University of Iowa. Then he took the Owls on an unlikely run to the NIT championship in 1969, when he defeated Eagles coach Bob Cousy in his final college game and broke the Eagles' nineteen-game winning streak.

Harry was part of the history of the game. Bill was just starting to make history.

Bill was the most organized person I had ever met. His attention to detail helped me later on when it came to running a business. He had everything down to the minute. So if you were going to do drills or someone like Bob Knight would come in to lecture, everything ran like clockwork. Harry lined up the speakers and Dick handled all the nuts and bolts, like registering everybody for camp and making sure the games on the outdoor courts ran on time.

Dick really opened my eyes. He was smart enough to say, "You've got some talent, but you're behind. You didn't make the team the first two years. You were skinny, and you finally gained enough weight." I was playing five or six hours a day, but he made me realize how hard I had to work to achieve my goals. I didn't have five seconds to breathe for a month. I had limited times to play. But if I didn't do all that, I never would have gotten my scholarship to Rutgers University.

I built up a lot of confidence that summer that would serve me well at Bonner and beyond. I had become much more outgoing. I wasn't as awkward. I felt I was a good player and I had a shot to earn a scholarship. I was competing very well against kids from all over the country, and I made the camp all-star team. We had teams from as far away as Ames, Iowa. I can remember playing against Brad Greenberg and Seth, his younger brother, who both were from Long Island, New York, and were working the camp circuit as counselors. Brad originally went to Washington State University to play for George Raveling, then transferred back to the East Coast to play for Jim Lynam at American University. Seth played for Al LoBalbo at Farleigh Dickinson University. Both got into coaching. Brad spent time as a GM with the Sixers. Seth currently works for ESPN as an analyst.

I also got a chance to work on my shooting with the legendary instructor Hank Slider. Hank helped Duke, Temple, Fordham University, Vanderbilt University, and Rutgers as a shooting coach. He worked with NBA stars like Julius Erving, Billy Cunningham, Karl Malone, Dominique Wilkins, Dave Cowens, and Doc Rivers. I discovered that shooting a basketball was a lot like hitting a golf ball. Once you learn the technique, it's all practice.

I spent five weeks working at the camp. One time, Bill called me into the office and told me Adolph Rupp was coming to lecture, and Bill wanted me to act as Adolph's personal valet. He had won over 850 games and four national championships, and this was one of his final years at University of Kentucky before he turned the program over to Joe B. Hall because the mandatory retirement age in Kentucky was seventy.

Adolph was sixty-eight and looked frail. I'd get his meals, his pills. Here's the funny part. Adolph was once out there demonstrating and was showing us the Kentucky offense. So, he asked me to come out there and play defense, and he was going to set a pick and I was supposed to get around him to guard my man. So, I went up to him. I didn't really hit him. I politely went around him, and he just ripped me. "Goddammit," he said. "If you set a pick like that on me, I'd knock you on your ass."

One minute he was coaching me like Pat Riley; the next minute I was back getting him coffee. It was one of the biggest thrills of my life. Once I got an autograph from John Wooden at the Final Four. And I had a chance to spend three or four days with Adolph Rupp. In my generation, they were the two greatest coaches in college basketball.

Years later, I was playing for Rutgers against Utah in the 1974 NIT Final Four. And I had my best game in college. I scored ten points and hit four field goals from what now would be considered three-point range. I was walking off the court and Adolph was at the Garden, and he said, "Nice game, kid." He didn't ask me what his next camp assignment was that day.

I got my first recruiting attention toward the end of camp. Bill brought guard Gary Brokaw and his New Brunswick High School team to scrimmage against the campers and counselors. Gary was one of the best players in the country, and he was Rutgers' number-one recruit.

I must have made an impression. After the game, Bill asked if I would be interested in coming to Rutgers. That same night, Lou Rossini from New York University, who was there, asked me if I would be interested in NYU.

It was all a little overwhelming. I had not started a high school varsity game yet, and I was already being recruited by college coaches.

When I got home, I continued going to the observatory and Drexel Hill elementary school, where I would play pickup games with some of the best local college players in the area, like Fran Dunphy of La Salle University and Tommy Inglesby and Eddie Hastings of Villanova. Howard Porter of Villanova, who was the Most Outstanding Player in the 1971 NCAA Final Four, even came over once for a run. By the end of the summer, I felt pretty good about my game.

When it came time to decide on a college, I went to Dick Bernhart for advice. He was frank. "Mike," he said, "you are not going to be a pro. You should go to a good school where you can play and get a good education."

So, I narrowed down my choices to four schools—Rutgers, NYU, Princeton, and the Naval Academy.

"We felt like we sort of had the inside track," says Dick Lloyd, who was Bill Foster's assistant at Rutgers. "Dick Bernhart trusted Bill from camp. We knew he could play and we felt Mike had a jump shot that was reminiscent of Bob Lloyd."

I was interested in Annapolis because I wanted to become a pilot. The Navy coaches sent me to Willow Grove Naval Air Station for an eye test, but I failed because I was color-blind. So, forget Annapolis. I had no interest in spending five years on a ship. I was really interested in NYU because my grandfather went there. I went to see NYU Violets play Temple at the Palestra. I really liked Lou Rossini, who coached Columbia University to a 20–0 regular-season record in a berth in the NCAA tournament in 1951, then took the Violets to the Final Four in 1960 and produced future pros like Cal Ramsey, Tom "Satch" Sanders, Happy Hairston, Barry Kramer, and Mal Graham. I might have gone there, but Rossini told me they were getting rid of Division I basketball, citing financial reasons, and he was retiring at the end of the 1971 season because they couldn't give any more scholarships. So, forget that. As for Princeton, I knew it didn't give athletic scholarships and my parents did not have the money for an Ivy League education.

So, the decision was made for me. And I'm glad it was. Rutgers offered me a need-based alumni scholarship. It was a good school, and Bobby Lloyd had gone there. So I jumped at it and committed before the season.

When I met coach Bill Foster at basketball camp, I realized he was the type of man I would like to become. He reminded me of the iconic Big 5 coaches, like Harry Litwack, Jack Kraft of Villanova, Jack Ramsay of Saint Joseph's, and Paul Westhead of La Salle. I knew I was never going to be a pro. I didn't have the speed. But earning a scholarship was a way to get four years of undergraduate education for free, and it opened the doors for me in the corporate business world. It opened doors that most people from Upper Darby never see.

Before I got to Rutgers, there was always a Scarlet Knights presence at my games. Dick Lloyd, Rutgers' assistant basketball coach, and Herb Carman, a teacher in the New Brunswick school district who was a Rutgers graduate and a close friend of the coaches', would drive to Philly, grab a milkshake, and head over to Bonner. I still remember the time Bill and Dick came down to watch my game against Saint Joseph's Prep with Mo Howard, who was the best player in the league as a junior and eventually signed with the University of Maryland. I picked that Sunday afternoon to have my best game. I scored thirty-one points. It's a good thing they didn't show up for our previous game against Cardinal O'Hara High School. I scored six and played poorly. If they had seen that game, I might have been in trouble.

When Dick was on the road, Herb would show up. I think he watched eighteen of my games my senior year, and we became good friends. Upper Darby was racially segregated at that point. Herb was the first black person ever to stay at my house. My father asked him if he wanted to have a drink. Herb was very comfortable with white people, and my dad wanted him to feel comfortable, so he drove him to the Blue Bell Inn near the airport. I think Herb was scared to death.

My senior year at Bonner was challenging. We had to replace all five starters. We were young and small. Mike Stack, our six-foot-four center, and our point guard, Ed Stefanski, were a year behind me. Mike was a great all-around player who was a good passer for a big man. Eddie was a talented point guard who had been recruited by Dean Smith of North Carolina on the recommendation of DeMatha High School coach Morgan Wooten.

"My father wanted me to go to Princeton and play for Petey Carril. Back then, if you grew up in Delaware County, everybody's dream was to play for a Big 5 school like Penn, Villanova, Saint Joseph's, La Salle, or Temple," Eddie recalls. "So, I went to Penn. And Mike [Stack] signed with Villanova. Michael was a good shooter on a team that lacked outside shooting. Mike and I were both good playmakers. So, he was the recipient of two guys who could get him the ball."

I never let the fact that I could not blow by people or dunk backwards deter me. I was always able to work on what I was good at. I focused on becoming a great shooter, not just a good one. I was always looking for ways to get better. When I was at summer camp, I sought out Hank Slider. "Hey," I said, "how can I make ninety-three out of a hundred free throws instead of shooting seventy percent from the line?" I did the same thing later on in business. I was always a good communicator. I was always good at relationships. I was always good at focusing on profitability and turning around businesses. I always tried to optimize my strengths. I knew I had weaknesses, but I never let them get in the way.

Mike and I both averaged double figures that year, and I felt I played my best in big games.

We started off great, beating North Catholic by twenty-five points. We rolled through the Northern Division of the Philadelphia Catholic League in preseason. Mike and I averaged double figures, as I said, but we didn't have much depth and lacked the consistency we'd had the previous year. We wound up 16–14 but finished in a tie for fourth in the Southern Division and missed a chance to go back to the Palestra when we lost to West Catholic in an elimination game.

Our team was haunted by tragedy. Joe Donnelly, one of our starting guards, who was one of the most popular funny guys in the school, died right after we graduated when the car he was driving hit a pole on the New Jersey Turnpike. And Mike Stack died of cancer at age fifty-one. When I look back at what happened at Bonner, I realize it fortified every-thing my parents wanted for me. I graduated in the top quarter of my class. I did fine on the college boards. I got my scholarship and the senior class medal, and I developed a strong sense of perseverance. I was always proud of the fact that for someone who got cut two years in a row, I went out and scored 450 points as a senior in the Catholic League, which was tough to play in because of all the Division I talent and all the tiny gyms.

We would play at Saint Thomas More High School and I would hit the ceiling with my jump shot. Roman Catholic had a tiny three-hundred-seat gym on the third floor, and they would open the doors on one side, so if you dove for a loose ball, you would be headed for the fire escape.

I didn't let getting cut or the negative things that happened to me affect my ability to do what I needed to do in the future. I was always focused on the goal of getting a college scholarship, because I needed one to go to college. Though I didn't get everything I wanted on every occasion, I learned to maximize each opportunity.

CHAPTER 3

Exploring New Horizons

Going to Rutgers, I realized my world was a lot bigger than I thought. Rutgers is a large state university located halfway up the Jersey Turnpike in New Brunswick, New Jersey. Originally chartered as Queen's College in 1766, it's the eighth-oldest college in the country. It had an undergraduate population of over twenty-five thousand when I attended, along with five campuses on either side of the Raritan River. It has great traditions and beautiful old buildings, dating back to Revolutionary War times. But it borders downtown New Brunswick, which at the time was a rundown part of the city, an example of urban blight before Johnson & Johnson opened its world headquarters there in 1983 and poured money into redevelopment.

When I enrolled at Rutgers University in the fall of 1971, it was in its final year as an all-male school. Women were at Douglass College, another campus up the road.

This was the first time I had been on my own, and it took me a while to adjust to the culture shock.

Rutgers was considered a public Ivy that encouraged liberal thinking. It had picked up the nickname "The Berkeley of the East" toward the end of the Vietnam War, because there was so much social unrest and racial tension. The antiwar movement wanted to abolish the Reserve Officers' Training Corps (ROTC), which had been mandatory for two years before the start of the war. And black student activist groups were pushing for more diversity at Rutgers and Douglass. There were demonstrations, teach-ins, and sit-ins.

It was a different time in America.

My family had a military background. My grandfather and my uncles all served in World War I. When I was growing up, I used to visit my uncle Charlie in West Philadelphia. He would show me his weapons collection from the war. I never knew my grandfather, but I was very fond of my uncles. My older brother, Brad, was in the Marines, and my younger brother, Bobby, eventually enlisted in the Army. I had a student deferment, and by the time I graduated, the draft had ended. To me, patriotism and our country were important. To this day, it is still difficult for me when people disrespect our flag. I would not trade America for any other country, and I've traveled around the world and seen other places up close.

I was at Rutgers for an education and to play basketball. When I was in high school, I was used to being in class with thirty-five kids I had seen at Mass the day before. They all knew me. Now, I was thrust into huge freshman lecture halls with two hundred other students I didn't know. They came from different backgrounds and religions. They were smart, had strong opinions, and marched to the beat of their own drums.

I formed my game plan early. I was conscientious about attending class, paying close attention to the lecturers, and taking notes. If I didn't, it would have been easy to fall behind. And the faculty at Rutgers didn't fool around. It didn't matter whether you were an athlete. They couldn't have cared less. Athletics was not a priority at the university.

It was tough to know where we stood in class. When I was a freshman, Rutgers did not give grades. The courses were so difficult, and it was a pass/fail system. The school didn't want to hurt anyone's chances of getting into graduate school. Bonner did a good job of preparing me, so I felt I wasn't behind, but I did feel the pressure of the workload. I was a political science major and history minor. I had one political science instructor my first semester who told us we had to read fourteen books in his class, basically a book a week.

I said, "What did he just say?"

Sometimes you could read CliffsNotes for basic courses, but for others, I had to read the books. And if I did not complete the book, I would read enough to know what was going on. Several of my professors made an impression on me. Dr. Richard McCormick was the state historian of New Jersey and taught American and New Jersey history. He was very prepared and knew what he was talking about. I also had Richard Lehne for political science. He used to work in Trenton, New Jersey, as a consultant for the state. He was big in public policy and an expert in waste management. I took his classes three times. From him I learned the value of being out in the field and writing papers on it.

He'd say, "Mike, go out to Franklin Township, analyze the solid-waste system, then come back and tell me what you think about it." So, I'd go out, talk to the people in the town, and get the information. He taught me how to write. One of the biggest problems in business is that most people don't know how to write. They can't even write a good memo. Years later, when I was at Xerox working for a senior vice president, I wrote every memo for him, then I'd take it back for corrections. If you are going to write a memo for a senior vice president, you'd better be prepared to write on a number of topics.

I ran into Professor Lehne at a football game years later and told him I had taken three of his classes, and thanked him for the impact he had made on my career. He died at age seventy-five in 2019.

Schoolwork could be overwhelming. But I knew I had a haven in basketball. I had gotten a taste of Rutgers basketball before I enrolled, watching the Scarlet Knights play their home games at the College Avenue gym.

One of the first people I met at Rutgers was Edward Bloustein, the recently appointed president. We bumped into each other in the locker room one day. He was shorter than me, and he had on a pair of sneakers. Ed had come from Bennington College, a selective liberal arts school in

Vermont that was founded as a women's college and didn't turn coed until 1969. He was an academic with Ivy League credentials. We started talking, and he told me he really liked sports. "It's a wonderful thing," he said.

Ed served as president of Rutgers for eighteen years before he died in 1989. In my opinion, he was the catalyst that helped transform the perception of the university from being a private liberal arts school to a major research university.

Bill Foster and Dick Lloyd did most of their recruiting in the Philadelphia suburbs and South Jersey. There were three key members of the basketball team when I started at Rutgers: John McFadden, a five-foot-nine senior from Cardinal O'Hara High School in Springfield, Pennsylvania, was the Rutgers point guard; six-foot-nine junior Gene Armstead from Penncrest High School in Media, Pennsylvania, was the starting center; and Steve Kaplan, a six-foot-six junior from Collingswood High School in South Jersey, was the starting forward. It made the team a little more familiar to me that I had read about some of the players in my local paper. The leading scorer on that team was Bob Wenzel, a senior guard and two-time MVP from West Islip High School on Long Island, who eventually came home to coach his alma mater and won a pair of Atlantic ten championships in 1989 and 1991, when the Scarlet Knights were invited to the NCAA tournament.

Rutgers had a good team in 1971. It didn't have any pros, but it had fundamentally sound mid major players who led the Knights to a 16–7 record and an NIT appearance. Though I only made two trips to see games at Rutgers University after committing to Rutgers while still in high school, they made quite an impression on me.

I went to a game where they beat Bobby Knight's Army team by twenty points. I'll never forget walking down to the locker room afterward and hearing a crash. I asked one of the Rutgers assistants what had happened.

"Their coach probably threw a chair into the wall," he said.

The other game, they almost beat Fordham, which was the best team in New York that year. Rutgers lost by four and the Barn (the gym at

Rutgers) was rocking. The place was always packed, and it was always loud. It was a huge home court advantage.

I was looking forward to jumping in with both feet. But my excitement dwindled when I attended the Rutgers basketball banquet after the season and Bill Foster, the guy who had recruited me, announced he was leaving for the University of Utah. I give Bill credit. He told me, "Mike, Rutgers is the right place for you. You ought to stay right here." I could barely imagine driving up the turnpike, let alone flying to Salt Lake City. I appreciated his comments. I wanted to be close to my parents and my buddies. Rutgers was the best of both worlds for me. It was away from home but close enough that my friends could come to home games and I could go home if I wanted. The school quickly moved to maintain continuity by naming Dick Lloyd as head coach.

Dick had graduated from Upper Darby High in 1958 and attended Bloomsburg State College as a walk-on, a non-scholarship player. He became one of the school's all-time great players and made the Associated Press All-State college team. He was also the class president during his junior and senior years.

Dick met Bill Foster before his junior year. Bill had just been hired after winning the Suburban I championship at Abington, and this was his first college coaching job. "The dean came up to me and told me we had just hired a new coach," Dick recalls. "I was the only guy from suburban Philly. Most of the guys were from Wilkes Barre and Scranton in Northeast Pennsylvania, and he asked if I would give him a tour of campus. The rest is history."

Dick had been Bill's right-hand man since 1963, when Bill moved to Rutgers. "The transition was easy for me since I played for him and used to work at his summer camp," Dick says. "I can remember playing in the scrimmages at night. I played against former NBA player and coach Gene Shue once, and he kept holding me to slow me down. He had his hand on my hip and I said, 'You can't do that.'

"'Where I play, you can do that,' he said. I remember John Havlicek coming as a counselor after his senior year at Ohio State before he became a Hall of Famer with the Celtics, and we'd go down to that little pond near the cabins and look for frogs," Dick continues. "John Wooden was a coach in residence for a week. George Raveling, one of the best recruiters in the country when he worked at Villanova, worked as a counselor. Jimmy Valvano were there, too.

"They had a memorial service for Bill at Rutgers, and during the eulogy I said, 'What would have happened if I hadn't met Bill Foster?'"

Dick hired John McFadden as the freshman coach; he would be my coach, as freshmen weren't eligible to play on the varsity team that year. Then, influential scouting guru Howard Garfinkel who owned and managed the famous Five-Star basketball camp convinced Dick to hire Dick Vitale, a local high school coach who had led East Rutherford High School to a pair of New Jersey Group I state titles, as his recruiter. "Dick had already interviewed six guys for the job," Vitale recalls. "But Mr. Garfinkel convinced him to talk to me. He told Dick Lloyd, 'If you interview him, you are going to hire him.' That's exactly what happened."

Dick Lloyd was big on conditioning for his players. We did a lot of running, much more than I had done in high school. I had to run a six-minute mile just to be on the freshman team. And I'm no miler. I think I came in at five minutes and fifty-eight seconds.

Expectations were high for the varsity team my freshman year. That was echoed by Ken O'Brien, who covered the team for the New Brunswick *Home News* and said the team would go 25–0. That was in part because of guard John Somogyi, a local hero from Saint Peter's of New Brunswick and the 1970 national Freshman of the Year at University of New Mexico who was transferring home. He averaged 33.4 points a game during his career at Saint Peter's and was the state's all-time leading scorer in high school with 3,310 points. He was a *Parade* All-American in 1968 and led Saint Peter's to a pair of state championships.

The first game I played for Rutgers was the freshman–varsity scrimmage. Here I was a few months out of high school, and I was playing against John Somogyi. Well, I scored seventeen points in the first half. John could shoot the lights out. He averaged twenty points the two years he played at Rutgers. But he wasn't the best defensive player.

I felt good after that game. I had played well in front of a packed house. But I remember thinking, "If I can get seventeen in a half against our varsity, how are we going to make it back to the NIT this year?"

We found out quickly how we compared to other teams. Princeton, our biggest rival, beat us by twenty-five points.

Three freshmen players had scholarships: Tony DiPaolo from Mount Saint Michael Academy in the Bronx, a six-foot-two point guard, a second team All-New York City player, and one of the toughest players I ever played against; Steve Brackbill, a six-foot-six left-handed forward from State College who was rail thin and played only one year before he left the program; and myself.

Tony and I averaged thirty-seven points between us, but we didn't have much size inside. And we were playing against guys like Kevin Washington and Joe Anderson of Temple, and George Bucci and Billy Campion of Manhattan College. I scored twenty-seven points against George as a freshman, and he later played in the NBA for a while. My team fared okay, but we had just as many losses as wins. I remember missing the first part of a one-on-one against Princeton at the end of a game in which we lost by a point.

At Rutgers, I was exposed to people I never had contact with while living in Upper Darby. I had an uncle who was an engineer on the Pennsylvania Turnpike, as I mentioned, but these people had a whole different level of success.

The first time I watched Rutgers play, I met Abe Suydam, who was a Rutgers grad, class of 1951, and was a huge donor. He loved the Rutgers basketball team, and he and his wife, Ann, were regulars at all the games. The MVP trophy is named after him.

Abe owned and operated a 380-acre farm in Somerset, seven miles from campus.

The farm had five homes on it. Abe was the president of the local bank, and his mother was on the board of the Franklin Insurance Company in Princeton. But he just seemed like a normal guy who loved farming. He also had a home on Long Beach Island and a condo in Jackson, Wyoming, and he traveled all over the world. I thought, "God, I want to be doing what this guy is doing. He's had a hell of a life."

And Abe was a very generous man. In fact, I lived in a three-bedroom apartment above his office, along with Tony DiPaolo and Jim Zielinski from our freshman team. He was a very generous man, and he was my landlord. I'd come home from practice, and I'd be exhausted and have something to eat. I'd visit him in his office, and we'd sit there talking about the business, the stock market, what was going on at his farm. I learned so much just from having a relationship with him. I didn't know anything about the stock market. I'd never owned a stock. So I was getting an education away from Rutgers that was pretty special—learning about business, learning how a different segment of society operated. He once took me to a French restaurant in Princeton, and I was like, "They have white tablecloths." I can remember it was a big deal when my parents had taken us to the Collegeville Inn for the smorgasbord.

And he knew everybody.

I got to meet Bruce Williams, who was the mayor of Franklin Township, New Jersey, and a famous radio announcer who ran an advice show on WMCA in New York City focused on personal business matters such as real estate transactions, career planning, entrepreneurship, and travel. I also met Floyd Bragg, who was a top executive at Prudential Financial, and David A. "Sonny" Werblin, an alum from Brooklyn who was a prominent music industry executive and sports impresario. Werblin was the owner of the New York Jets and chairman of Madison Square Garden, and had built and managed the Meadowlands Sports Complex in New Jersey. He and Williams had huge jobs.

At the end of our freshman year, Tony and I felt we had a chance to play as sophomores. Rutgers was graduating a lot of seniors.

That summer, I suggested a road trip to the state of North Carolina, and we played against my brother Brad, who was on the All-Marine basketball team at Camp Lejeune. We would play games against the Marines. They would beat the heck out of us, throw us on the floor. We would be sitting on the beach and there would be a lot of Marines running by with their drill sergeants. It was an eye-opening experience for college kids to see that and know we were still at war.

My future did not play out as envisioned, because my skills did not equal Dick Vitale's recruiting ability. I liked Dick from the beginning He had a great personality. A lot of people thought he was phony, because he talked so much. But that was Dick. It was hard not to be captivated by his passion for the sport. He loved sports trivia. We would sit on the bus and talk sports trivia. He would talk 80 percent of the time and you would talk twenty percent of the time. If you couldn't accept it, that was your problem.

Dick dreamed that Rutgers could be a Top ten program competing for a national championship, but it had settled for mediocrity.

"I wanted to recruit the best of the best," he recalls. "And Dick [Lloyd] gave me the leeway to do it. I always felt Rutgers had a mindset of, 'We're Rutgers; we can't go after this kid and that kid. My feeling was, 'Why couldn't you?' Rutgers was a good school academically. You were close to recruiting hotbeds in Philly, New Jersey, and New York. You got Madison Square Garden. I thought there was a lot to sell, and I built up a lot of contacts through coaching in Jersey and running camps there."

Dick's first recruiting target was Phil Sellers from Thomas Jefferson High School in Brooklyn, a six-foot-five forward who had over two hundred offers and was considered the best prospect in the country. "He was the shining light in the New York area, and people kind of laughed at first" about Rutgers trying to recruit him, Dick says.

But Dick was a relentless recruiter during an era when there were no rules about how many times you could see a kid in person. "I must have driven to Jefferson thirty times," he recalls. "Phil was thinking Notre Dame, thinking Marquette but I was in there selling the idea of him being a star in his hometown and playing in the Garden."

The summer after my freshman year, I saw firsthand Dick's energy and why he was a successful recruiter. I was shooting around at the Barn. Dick brought Phil Sellers to campus for an unofficial visit, and Phil had two guys with him from Brooklyn. We got some guys from the varsity and arranged for a pickup game. All of a sudden, a guy was driving past me, and he dunked the ball over his shoulder. I said to Dick, "Who the hell is that guy?" And he said, "That's Lloyd B. Free. The other guy is Fly Williams. All three of them are pros." So, Dick had Fly Williams, Phil Sellers, and Lloyd Free. Fly played for Madison High and set all kinds of scoring records at Austin Peay State University and played for Saint Louis in the old American Basketball Association (ABA). Free went to Guilford College from Canarsie High School, then played multiple years in the league with the Philadelphia 76ers and San Diego. And Phil Sellers was the best player in the country,

And they were all playing against me in the gym.

And I said to Dick, "If these guys come, I'm never going to play." He said to me, "Don't worry, I may only get one."

It was funny, but I wasn't laughing.

It was a difficult time for me but one of the things I had to get through. Dick recruited Ron Williams, a six-foot-two guard from Washington, D.C., and Admiral Farragut Academy in New Jersey; guard Mike Dabney from East Orange High School; six-foot-seven forward Bruce Scherer from Parsippany Hills High School in New Jersey; six-foot-seven Mike Palko from Hackettstown High School in New Jersey; and Phil.

Dick was always welcoming. He invited me on one of his many trips to recruit Phil. We drove up to Phil's neighborhood in Brooklyn. I remember saying to him, "That's a rough neighborhood." It was much different from the banks of the Raritan or Upper Darby.

So, off we went. When we got to the apartment where Phil lived, Dick gave money to a kid on the street so they would not steal his car. We took the elevator upstairs; everyone thought we had to be coaches when they saw us walking in with our overcoats. We went in and Dick said, "You know more about the academics. So, you handle that part. I'll talk about basketball."

So, I was over in one corner, talking to Phil's mother about how Rutgers isn't a basketball factory, and how Bill Foster graduated almost 100 percent of his players, and how guys like Bob Lloyd were CEOs of their own companies. And Dick was talking to Phil, telling him how great it would be to play in the Garden and if he came, Rutgers would be going to the Final Four.

Dick was a great salesman and he always gave his best, but it looked like he was going to come up short when Phil called later and told him he was going to the University of Notre Dame. His ego was smooshed. "I felt in my heart that wasn't what he wanted," Dick says. "But he was experiencing a lot of peer pressure between faculty, teammates, and guys in the neighborhood. When he told me, I congratulated Phillip and wished him good luck."

Two weeks later, Dick was at a postseason all-star game between the Public Schools Athletic League (PSAL) and the Catholic League. He was recruiting Jeff Kleinbaum, a tough guard who played for Marv Kessler at Martin Van Buren High School in Queens. Dick was sitting in the stands with scout Howard Garfinkel when Phil came over and asked Dick to stay around after the game because he wanted to talk to him. As it turned out, Phil had had a change of heart. "Phil the Thrill" decided to come to Rutgers. It was one of the few schools that could make it happen since it did not subscribe to the national letter of intent. One small problem: Rutgers didn't have a scholarship available. "We got [the scholarship] done the next day," Dick says.

"I couldn't say no to Dick," Phil admits. "He had been there every day, and I trusted him. Plus, I thought I could play right away at Rutgers."

That was the turning point of Rutgers' going from a team with basically three-star players to a team filled with four- and five-star players.

It kick-started Rutgers' best year ever recruiting. Phil Sellers was a pied piper. Mike Dabney was the best player in New Jersey. He was one of the fastest players I had ever seen, and he was graceful on the court. If you were out on the fast break, there was nobody better. He had no interest in Rutgers at first. But as soon as he found out Phil was coming, he jumped on the bandwagon, which was getting crowded. Mike Palko could rebound and block shots. Bruce Scherer was a big body. Jeff Kleinbaum, who also signed, was a tough defender, and Ron Williams was a big-time shooter. Phil and Mike Dabney always seemed to come up big in big games. So, you had two guys who had great confidence in themselves.

The campus was energized. Freshmen became eligible to play varsity in 1973, and Dick Lloyd and Dick Vitale wanted to keep that six-man group together. Tony DiPaolo also moved up to varsity, because they needed his position more. You could have argued I was as good as some of those guys, but the reality was that I knew my minutes would have been limited. I chose to play on the JV team. The rest of the campus saw the varsity team's jumping into the national spotlight and possibly making the thirty-two-team NCAA tournament.

I went to the Gator Bowl, and I dressed when we made the NIT. But I was still playing for John McFadden, along with a lot of players from the 1972 freshman team, plus Pete Clark, a tight end in football who was a six-foot-two center. I lit it up that season, averaging 32.7 points, and I had forty or more five times. We ended up 15–3. We used to play prelims before the varsity games, and most of our games were packed in the second half. Hey, I really liked the fact that I got to play. I went from averaging fourteen points a game my senior year at Bonner to seventeen a game as a Rutgers freshman to thirty-two a game as a sophomore, so I really got much better as a player.

I loved playing for John, our coach. He had once been a classic overachieving point guard who had been heavily recruited by all the Big 5 schools as a junior, but he slipped off the radar after he broke his right elbow in a summer league game. He missed the next three months. "I played most of my senior year left-handed," he recalls. "I shot my free throws left-handed. I did everything left-handed. I went to Rutgers because of Dick Lloyd. He watched me play in some high-level pickup games with his brother in Drexel Hill before I got hurt, and I must have made an impression. When other schools faded away, Rutgers filled the void.

"Dick saw me play at the Coatesville Tournament my senior year. He still talks about it. I shot seven for eleven from the line, shooting left-handed, and he said to my father, 'We really need him to work on his free throw shooting.' My father said to him, 'Well, if he shoots them right-handed, he ought to be able to do that.'"

John was a three-year starter and had a great basketball IQ. He worked at Rutgers for six years after he graduated, and I believe he would have made a great head coach if he hadn't decided to go into private business with Merrill Lynch. He certainly knew how to feature me in the offense. "Mike could really shoot the ball," John recalls of my playing. "I'm a big believer if God gives you lemons, make lemonade. I coach a girls' AAU [Amateur Athletic Union] team these days, and I tell them, 'God did not create everybody equal. Some of you are going to get more looks and touches. Some of you are going to have to guard and rebound. This is not an equal opportunity sport when everybody gets to jack it up.'

"We went fifteen and three [during] Mike's sophomore year with an amalgamation of players. I would sit there and wonder how we were going to win a game with this group. We weren't very good, but Michael could really shoot. It's easy to coach bad players. It's the good players who are harder to coach, because egos get in the way. You know: 'Why him? Why not me?' When kids know they are just okay, they do whatever you tell him. We had a bunch of kids like that, and it was pretty easy to run sets, run screens, and get Mike the ball."

I could score. If you talk to Phil Sellers or Mike Dabney, they will tell you they couldn't leave me open in practice. But having to play JV was very frustrating, because here I was coming off a very good freshman year, and all of a sudden they dumped six freshmen ahead of me. It was hard to deal with. But I think getting cut from the team for two years and dealing with so much adversity in high school and having to work my way up got me through it and allowed me to think positively about it.

One thing that served me well in basketball as well as business: I realized I had to find my role on the team. Dick Lloyd finished his second year 15–11, and the pressure was so great. Some of the fans were so mean, his wife was crying in the stands. It was a difficult scenario. The varsity team did not lack talent, but the chemistry was a problem. The younger players were as good as the older players, and everybody was learning how to play together.

The stress of the job got to Dick Lloyd. The expectations surpassed the reality. Dick resigned in the middle of the 1973 season before a season-ending NIT loss to University of Minnesota. Dick eventually became the school's alumni director and stayed in that job until he retired. "He recommended me for the head coaching job," Dick Vitale says. "The players wanted me, too. I went in to see [Athletic Director] Fred Gruninger, but he wanted a big name and he was going after some big guys. What he told me was that he was going to make sure whoever was hired, they had to keep me on as an assistant. But I told him, 'If I don't get the head coaching job, if I'm not good enough, I'm leaving. I'm going somewhere else.' Then I made a big mistake. I told him, 'I don't want no raise. Just pay me what I was making as an assistant—eleven thou. Give me a one-year contract, and if I don't do the job, you're home free.' I felt if I got the job, I could turn it into a multiyear contract. I really felt Rutgers was a sleeping giant. But it didn't happen."

Dick left for the head coaching job at the University of Detroit, where he coached four pros and led the Titans to the NCAA Sweet Sixteen in 1977 before taking the head coaching job with the NBA's Detroit Pistons. Jimmy Valvano, a Rutgers alum who was coaching Bucknell University, was also interested in being the Rutgers head coach, but he was too flamboyant for Gruninger. Eventually Rutgers hired Tom Young from American University, and the search committee included Phil Sellers and Mike Dabney.

I was fortunate that everyone from university presidents to ambitious coaches and successful businessmen reinforced the importance of hard work, what enthusiasm and vision can do, and how the best-laid plans often require adjustment. Rutgers opened my world in every way, and I was still a student. Everyone took on the role of professor, and I was the consummate student.

CHAPTER 4

Finding Ways to Stay Relevant

With Dick Lloyd gone, Fred Gruninger wanted someone with established head coaching experience. He got lucky when he selected Tom Young from American University. Tom had played for Bud Millikan at the University of Maryland, a disciple of Naismith Hall of Fame coach Henry Iba. Bud was an All-American when he played for Henry at Oklahoma A&M and was his assistant when the Oklahoma A&M Cowboys won the 1945 and 1946 NCAA championship. Bud coached at Maryland for seventeen years, from 1950 to 1967, and won an Atlantic Coast Conference (ACC) title in 1958. Every senior who played for him graduated, and he was a huge believer in discipline. His players were required to wear team blazers while traveling, and during warm-ups players wore towels around their neck in an ascot-like manner.

Some of that rubbed off on Tom when he was Millikan's assistant at Maryland. At American, Tom coached Kermit Washington, a first-team All-American big man who eventually played in the NBA and was coming off a 1973 NIT appearance.

It took a while for Tom to decide whether or not to coach for Rutgers, because there was a perception that the team's lack of success the previous year had been caused by racial tensions that were also prevalent on the campus. And, like so many other coaches knew, you could not win big there. But it was his friend Bob Knight who convinced him the program could be a sleeping giant.

Tom was willing to see for himself. He saw it as a good next step for him professionally, and he brought his able assistants Joe Boylan and Art Perry. He also retained John McFadden as the freshman/JV coach. Securing Joe was a real coup, as he had been offered the American head coaching job, but he passed because he was loyal to Tom and saw the opportunity as well. He also was reluctant to surrender his summers, as he was the captain of the Stone Harbor, New Jersey, beach patrol. Joe was one of the great people in basketball. He treated the players well. He handled more than x's and o's. He made sure everyone succeeded on the court and in the classroom. He fit Rutgers like a glove.

Tom, on the other hand, ruled with an iron fist. He was a tough coach and a tough guy. His practices were two hours of nonstop running. He had one drill that involved running the length of the court six times in twenty-four seconds.

And we'd better not be late.

There was never a doubt that Tom was in control. He knew how he wanted things done. Defense was one of them. He was a man-to-man defensive coach, and if you didn't play defense his way, you didn't play. He was a man of principles.

Coaches today have a huddle with their assistants before they have a huddle with the team, trying to decide what to tell the players. That was never the case with Tom. He always made the call. Everyone knew Tom's decisions were final.

Tom's first big victory came before the season started. He needed Phil Sellers to understand the way he wanted him to play. Phil had been the leading scorer the previous year. A lot of coaches try to coddle players. That is not how Tom handled his business. In fact, Tom threw Phil out of practice on a couple of occasions. One time when Phil and a younger forward named Hollis Copeland almost came to blows, Tom told the two of them to go downstairs to the locker room if they wanted to fight. They eventually reemerged and watched the rest of practice in the stands.

"When I went to Rutgers," Tom recalls, "I had heard all about the tension between the players and coaches. People told me it would make a hard job even more difficult. As soon as I arrived, it was obvious Phil wanted to call his own shots. As soon as I arrived, it was important to have Phil understand his role on the team. I had to throw him out of practice a couple of times. I told him, 'Let me tell you something. I'm going to be here four years. I just got a new contract. I don't know how long you are going to be here. You're either going to play our way or you're not playing. You go get a shower.'"

Each time, Phil came back contrite. "The thirteen other guys noticed what you did to the best player on the team," Tom recalls. "It's not like I chased the twelfth guy off. I think most of the guys were happy to see Phil get shut down every once in a while. It helped Phil. To his credit, he became a good teammate and a great player."

There was no denying Phil's talent. He averaged 23.2 points and 9.4 rebounds and had some huge games as a junior. He scored forty-three against USC, forty against Columbia, and thirty-four against Navy, and scored twenty-five or more points a dozen times. And this was without a three-point play or a shot clock.

Tom wanted to play uptempo, and we had a team that was perfectly suited for it once Eddie Jordan joined the roster. Eddie, who had played for Archbishop Carroll High School in Washington, D.C., was the leader we had been looking for. He originally had signed to play for Tom at American, then got a release and followed him to the Banks (Rutgers University). He and Phil hit it off right away. They both wanted to win, and they respected each other's talent. I too realized how good Eddie was, as I played against him one-on-one almost every day.

I quickly realized that my contribution to the team would not come in minutes played.

Eddie had a great personality and was a good leader, and we hit it off right away. I remember the first time I saw him play. I had Nicky Cangi and some of my buddies up at Rutgers when Eddie was a freshman. Nick said to me, "Boy, he doesn't shoot very well." I said to him, "One day, he's going to play in the NBA. I haven't seen many guys quicker than him." I knew from the first day. And he was good. Eddie understood that his role was running the team, and he distributed the ball as well as anyone. Tom also realized his ability. When we got a rebound, the only person we could throw it to was Eddie. Eddie would go to the ball, and Mike Dabney and Phil, who were great finishers, would take off. It was one of the reasons we had a great fast break. Eddie would get the ball, and he could beat anybody off the dribble and hit those guys on the wing.

Our starting lineup my junior year was Phil, Mike Dabney, Eddie, senior power forward Vinnie Roundtree from New Jersey, and Mike Palko. Freshman guard Mark Conlin, a lockdown defensive player from Bishop Reilly High School in Queens who was the only married player on the team, was the sixth man. Mark originally had committed to Boston College but wound up at Rutgers off a recommendation from Howard Garfinkel after Boston College reneged on the scholarship offer because it had signed two other guards.

We raced through an 18–8 season and earned an invitation to the NIT, where we lost to our former coach Bill Foster and his Utah team, 102–89, in a second-round game at the Garden. We were fun to watch. We averaged eighty-seven points.

This was Phil's team now, and these were his players. And he could be relentless in practice. I know. I had to guard him. "I felt bad for Mike MacDonald," Mark says. "Phil would just destroy guys."

"There was a lot of pressure playing for Rutgers," Phil recalls. "So many people in my neighborhood questioning my decision: 'Why did you pick Rutgers? Where's Rutgers?' I wanted to prove them wrong and show I could take Rutgers places they had never been."

The peer pressure combined with the racial tension on university campuses put Phil in the middle of everything. Many black students on campus were becoming frustrated by their economic conditions, which were not improving despite the gains of the civil rights movement. We experienced it firsthand during our second game of the year during my junior year. We were playing a good Pittsburgh team, the Panthers, at the sold-out Barn. With three minutes left in the half, the Panthers were leading, 36–21. During a timeout, a group of students marched onto the basketball court and staged a demonstration to protest the fact that they felt black faculty and staff were not being compensated fairly.

Hal Grossman, a veteran referee who was the head official, said if the demonstrators did not clear the court in twenty minutes, Rutgers would have to forfeit. They did not leave. The game was called off, and the Panthers were awarded a 2–0 win. It is still one of the few forfeits in the history of college basketball.

During the demonstration, Phil got on the public address system, urging the students to leave the court. "We've worked so hard for this," he said. He felt the team was a good representative of the university.

We never let it affect us, though. The tension off the court never affected the team. We had six black players and six white players, and we were close. We never saw color or race. Phil Sellers, Mike Dabney, and Eddie Jordan were our best players and our leaders. And they never took a day off. Phil had tremendous basketball IQ. He could make passes. I would be open sometimes, and he'd make a pass that hit me in the head because I didn't think it could get to me. So many times, we had to be aware or we'd look foolish. Phil pushed our team the same way I saw Michael Jordan push the Chicago Bulls in the documentary *The Last Dance*.

We played against some great players like Billy Knight, Lou Dunbar of University of Houston, Gus Williams of USC, Dennis DuVal of Syracuse University, and Joe Bryant of La Salle University, and we got some good wins. We defeated Princeton, Oklahoma State, Syracuse, Penn State, West Virginia, and Saint Bonaventure. Phil, Mike Dabney, Eddie, and Vinny all averaged in double figures. The rest of us were role players who averaged three or four points a game.

I played in thirteen games that year, shot seventeen for thirty-five and averaged three points a game, but our second team was always competitive in scrimmages. This was an important life lesson, that top players need to be challenged by the bench, and it served me well in my professional career when I realized my name wouldn't be called in the NBA draft.

But I did get my moment to shine in our NIT loss to Utah in the world's greatest arena.

We were down seventeen with six minutes to play when Tom put me in and told me to start shooting. "We got to catch up," he said.

I scored a quick ten points, and I think I was five for seven. And four of my field goals were from long range. Madison Square Garden was a great place to play. It was probably the best place to play for a shooter because of the background. And I had a green light.

The euphoria of the season didn't last long for me.

After the season, I came down with mono. I wasn't feeling well, and the Rutgers doctors didn't pick it up. So, I went back to Upper Darby and saw my family doctor, and he diagnosed it. I had to stay in bed for six weeks. I left school and Jean Murock—a pretty, popular young woman who was Tom's basketball secretary and ran the office—made sure I had all my assignments sent to me, and I would do all my schoolwork from home. I didn't know then that she was going to be my best teammate ever.

The one thing that saved me during those six weeks was the Philadelphia Flyers' run to the Stanley Cup. All of those ice hockey games were on an old UHF channel, and I watched every game with Bobby Clarke and Bernie Parent. If I hadn't had that diversion, I think I would have gone crazy. I was sick as a dog, with bloody noses. The other thing was, I wasn't allowed to play basketball after I got over the mono until the following September.

But I went back to campus in the summer and had the opportunity to work at the bankers' convention that was hosted by Rutgers every year. I used to run one of the dormitories for all these guys who would come to campus during the summer for seminars. Then I'd go work the basketball camps. I worked for Billy Cunningham, Walt Frazier, Dave Cowens, Speedy Morris, and Jim Valvano.

Going into my senior year, I figured I had a chance to play more because we had just lost two guards, Ronnie Williams and Tony DiPaolo, who left the team because they weren't getting enough playing time. But I quickly learned I had to manage expectations.

Rutgers signed a great six-foot-six forward named Hollis Copeland from Ewing High School in New Jersey, who was a high jumper who ran the floor like a deer. And it also brought in Steve Hefele from East Rockaway, a six-foot-five shooting guard whom I felt could have been the next Geoff Petrie, the Princeton great. Hollis became an immediate starter at forward, replacing Vinnie Roundtree, and Tom alternated Mike Palko and Les Cason, a six-foot-ten high school All-American from North Jersey who had played for Dick Vitale in high school, at center.

As soon as I started playing pickup games with Steve, I realized he was going to take whatever minutes I had thought I was going to get. To make matters worse, early in preseason practice, we were running a suicide drill and I broke my left wrist.

I talked with Tom after practice, and he asked me if I still wanted to play. I said yes.

Then he told me I wasn't going to be getting the minutes with Steve on the roster.

"Look, Tom," I said. "I have no issue with the role I'm going to play. I'll help you in practice. I want to play and finish out my four years."

Tom was fine with it. The thing I respected most about Tom was that I always knew where I stood with him.

Think about it. If I had my role in today's game, the coaches would be trying to get me to leave so they could get another scholarship player. If you are the ninth or tenth guy on the team, you are expendable. The difference in those days was that players stayed for four years and there was a relationship between a coach and a player. If you were loyal and did the right things, coaches respected it.

I saw that at other schools. I worked with a guy named Woody Coley, who played for Dean Smith at North Carolina. He was the same type of player as me. He played in practice. But Dean never thought about asking him to leave, either.

In the end, I looked at it realistically. I felt this was going to be one of the best basketball teams I would ever be on. I thought we really were going to be good. Rutgers had never made the NCAA tournament. But this team was good enough. "I have a chance to be on the greatest team in school history," I thought.

I always put value on being part of a winning team. I wasn't going to transfer to a school like Bucknell or Lafayette with less than a year to graduate just so I could average fifteen or twenty points a game. I made a decision that playing with better players would give me more satisfaction. It was almost like my junior year at Bonner. I learned so much playing against the varsity. Those guys were good players, and I had the same experience playing against Phil, Dabney, Eddie, and Hollis in practice. I was playing against guys who were at the level of the best players in college basketball, and it was fun. I remember we would be playing against a team like Syracuse, which had a terrific shooter in Greg Coles. And Tom would say to me, "You're Greg Coles in our scrimmage." So, I would go out there and Eddie and Dabney would chase me around, and I got to put up thirty shots. Even though I didn't get to play as much as other people, I think my courage was a big contributor—my being able to deal with getting cut at Bonner all those years, and then going to Rutgers and playing behind very good players and never quitting. That helped me later, too, when I went into the workforce competing against Ivy League graduates.

I think Tom always felt I had a good attitude. I was not a guy who was going to cause a lot of headaches for the coaches, and I was a good shooter. If Steve did go down, I figured I could come in and fill his role.

"At Rutgers, we used to run the ball down the floor, look for a three-on-two and try to get a layup from the right or left side, depending on how good the point guard was," Tom says. "Now, one guy goes to the hole, one guy sits in the middle, and one guy goes to the corner. That would be Mike MacDonald, sticking the three. Unfortunately, Mike was fifteen years ahead of his time."

Tom offers a memory: "We're playing Carolina when I was at Old Dominion, and they had just put in the three-point line in 1986. We used to go inside to the big guy, and if we didn't get that, we would get it out to the three-point line for a jumper. So, we're playing Carolina right after Christmas, and they had just come back from Hawaii. Dean Smith was one of the great coaching minds out there. I looked at some film and figured they wouldn't change. Coming into the game, their guards were taking four or five shots a game. When they played us, the guards took 50 percent of the shots from beyond the arc."

We played an inside-out game. I was unfortunate in that my style of play probably would have better in today's world, where you come down and take twenty-five-foot jump shots and you don't worry about it. In those days, if we had taken a twenty-five-footer, Tom might have had a heart attack. When I played for Tom, we played intense man-to-man defense and got a lot of steals; the pressure was intense. If I played Eddie Jordan one-on-one from the foul line, I could beat him. But with full-court man-to-man pressure, if I played against Eddie, I would have problems getting the ball up the floor. Our guys were so quick.

So, the 1975 season started, and we did have a heck of a team.

We played our opening game against University of Hawaii in Honolulu, and we beat them. Our football team was out there at the same time playing Hawaii. So, I got to spend a week in Hawaii hanging out with teammates and other friends from campus. I was playing football on the beach in Honolulu with the football players. That was also the week that Mark Conlin's wife, Kathleen, had a baby. He missed the birth because we went right from Hawaii to play Utah and couldn't see her until we got back. Later on he was home visiting his wife one time, but he was late for practice because he had a flat tire. When he went to apologize to Tom, Tom gave him a stern look. "Having a baby gives you certain perks," he said. "Missing practice is not one of them."

We beat Saint John's and Princeton for a second straight year—and three teams from the fabled Big 5. We beat Temple by fifteen, La Salle at the Palestra by fifteen, and Saint Joseph's by thirty. For me, that was heaven. After the La Salle game, my mother had the entire team over to the house.

We beat Syracuse the year they went to the Final Four. Eddie stole the ball with five seconds left, and we won by a point at Manley Field House. It was one of the few times the Scarlet Knights won at Manley or the Carrier Dome. And we did it in a hostile environment. The students at the game were out of control. They were throwing pennies at us during the entire game. "They threw a quarter at me," Phil remembers. "Then they were trying to steal our warm-ups. Our trainer, Andy Sivess, was ready to fight the entire student body."

One day my father said to me, "Why aren't you playing ahead of those guys?"

I said, "Dad, these guys—Phil, Dabney, Eddie—are going to be pro players. I play with them every day." I was realistic about my own abilities and aware of how hard I needed to work. Being effective at anything you have to know what you can do and work at it.

Then we won at West Virginia, beating the Mountaineers 86–84 in double overtime against a team featuring Bob Huggins. I'd like to think my efforts in practice were evident that day as Steve Hefele hit three shots—two to send the game into overtime and one to win the game.

Though it was a great season, it was not a perfect season.

We played USC in the Holiday Festival Classic at the Garden and the big matchup was Eddie Jordan against Gus Williams. We used to call Eddie "Fast Eddie," but Gus Williams, the schoolboy legend from Mount Vernon, New York, was not going to let us beat him in his backyard. Eddie was dribbling up the floor and Williams stole the ball at half court. Eddie was a great defensive player. But Williams was so quick, he was going in for a layup and Eddie still hadn't hit the foul line.

Tom called a timeout, and I said, "Eddie, you aren't Fast Eddie anymore."

To earn an automatic bid to the thirty-two-team NCAA tournament that year, Rutgers first had to qualify by playing in one of four four-team Eastern College Athletic Conference (ECAC) tournaments. We were paired with Saint John's, Seton Hall, and Saint Peter's at the Garden. We beat Saint Peter's easily, then drew Saint John's in the final.

St. John's was our biggest rival at the time. We wanted to play them. We had a lot of guys from New York City.

The game was played in front of only 7,294 fans, because of a mistaken announcement by NBC that it would be carried in the New York area. Despite the lack of fans, we knew what was at stake. It was as competitive a game as we had played all year. Phil had twenty-two, and Hollis Cope-land and Eddie both had nineteen, but we were down ten points with thirteen minutes and forty seconds to play. We rallied to send the game into overtime when Eddie hit a jumper to tie the game at 69–69 with eleven seconds remaining in regulation. Saint John's was up 77–74 with just two minutes and twenty-seven seconds to go in overtime before Phil hit a jumper from the key (the circle above the foul line) and Eddie scored on a layup to give us a one-point lead, then Phil grabbed a huge rebound off a miss by Mel Utley and Saint John's was forced to foul, and Eddie gave us a two-point lead when he made the first of two free throws with twelve seconds to play.

Rutgers was going to the big dance for the first time ever.

The NCAA selection committee didn't do us any favors. They sent us to Oral Roberts University in Tulsa, Oklahoma, to play a first-round game against Louisville, which had Junior Bridgeman, Allen Murphy, and Phil Bond. The Mabee Center at Oral Roberts is one of those arenas where the court is elevated. We got there for a practice the day before our game, and the university's namesake, televangelist Oral Roberts, had a big convention going on—ten thousand people. He had singers and a band. Like most Pentecostal ministers, the guy performed like a rock star, and there is no doubt that the money collection was much bigger than it ever had been at Saint Laurence.

Then, we played in the game. We hung in there for a while. We were within eight points after thirty minutes. But we lost 94–78. We were worn out. They had a monster bench, and Bridgeman went off for thirty-eight points. Six of his shots had to be from three-point range. They were really good. They advanced to the Final Four before losing by two points in overtime to John Wooden's last NCAA championship team at UCLA in the national semifinals at San Diego.

Who knows how good we might have been if Les Cason had become the player everyone thought he would become?

Les transferred to Rutgers from San Jacinto Junior College in January 1974. He'd played for Dick Vitale at Rutherford High, and when he was a tenth grader, he was drawing comparisons to Willis Reed. He wound up becoming the second-all-time leading scorer in the state, and his high school team was 29–0 and the Group I state champion when he was a senior. Les was a nice kid, but I quickly realized when I was tutoring him that he didn't have the same fundamentals the Augustinians taught at Bonner.

Les was a great shooter, not just a good shooter. But I'm not sure he enjoyed the competition. He laid an egg at the Dapper Dan Roundball Classic, scoring just two points. Jerry Tarkanian, the Hall of Fame coach from the University of Nevada, Las Vegas, who was at California State University Long Beach at the time, offered him a scholarship but eventually withdrew it. I had dinner with Jerry when I was at Xerox. Jerry said he had recruited Les off his reputation. But it all fell apart quickly when Les scored only two points in the Dapper Dan. "Les came to Long Beach for a visit and stayed on the beach for two weeks," Jerry says. "He just wasn't tough enough to compete with our guys."

It reinforced the idea that your reputation may precede you, but you still have to produce. Les never averaged more than five points in his two and a half years at Rutgers.

"We were lucky enough to have two big guys, James and Roy Hinson, who were first-round picks in the NBA draft," Tom Young says. "Les was as talented as any of those guys. He was a nice guy, knew the game. He was a good shooter, a good passer. But he never learned how to stay focused.

"We were playing in the Garden, and I told Joe Boylan [assistant basketball coach at Rutgers] we were distributing their Pell Grant money. Les lived about an hour away. I told Joe, 'Make sure nobody gets their money until after we get on the bus.' So, we go to the Garden and Les is not on the bus. We go in the Garden and here's Les, walking around the Garden on the three level; he's got a nice new hat on, a new topcoat and gloves. I said, 'Go get Les!' He's already spent his Pell Grant money on clothes. That was Les." Sadly, Les's life eventually spiraled out of control after he left school. He wound up living in a park near the Battery in New York City and died of a drug overdose.

I enjoyed my time at Rutgers. I got a good education, graduated with a degree in political science, and can still remember the names of my professors. I also learned some life lessons. I think the values you have in everything you do help determine your success. Compromising your values is something that I never did in the classroom and that our team never did on the court.

I was lucky. I had a lot of role models and they weren't just the coaches, as I mentioned.

The support staff at Rutgers was wonderful. We had a team dentist, Dr. Joel Fertig. I didn't have any money when I was a kid. I went to the dentist only when I had a toothache. I didn't go for checkups. My parents couldn't afford it. When I got to Rutgers, my teeth weren't in the greatest condition. When I was playing, he took care of any problems with them. When I got married and had children, I would still go to him, and even though I had dental benefits from Xerox, he would not charge me.

I finally told him, "I have the money. I can pay you. My stock at Xerox is doing very well." He finally accepted it.

More important, I began dating Jean Murock. Jean grew up in South River, New Jersey, as an only child. Her father, Ed, was a former high school basketball star and a paratrooper in World War II who later became a truck driver and dispatcher. Her mom, Honora Murock, was an executive secretary at The Squibb Corporation (later Bristol-Myers Squibb). And her high school class included future NFL stars Joe Theismann and Drew Pearson. The family had been Rutgers fans for thirty years.

Jean had attended secretarial school before she took a job in the basketball office. She was good at her job. Our first date wasn't really a date. I asked her if she would come with me to my good friend Nick Cangi's wedding as a friend.

No matter how much I learned at Rutgers, I still didn't know how to dress for success, and I'm pretty sure I never impressed Jean with my clothes. "When I first met Mike," she remembers of me, "I think he had two pairs of jeans, sneakers, and a green corduroy sports jacket." But we found we had a lot in common. We both liked to play golf and liked the Jersey Shore, and she was a sports fan. She even went with me to some games when I was scouting for Jim Valvano at Iona University as a graduate assistant coach.

Though I didn't get the minutes on the basketball court, I still got the girl. And we're still relevant today.

CHAPTER 5

Near Perfection

Playing on an NCAA tournament team would be considered the high point of every college basketball player's career. In my senior year, I did just that. But I've always wanted to take one more shot and lace up again. Everything Bill Foster and Dick Lloyd told me about when they were recruiting me happened in part because of the efforts of Tom Young and his staff. As good as I thought the Scarlet Knights were, it was hard to imagine what the next year would hold for them.

The 1975–1976 season was magical, and to this day it's the high point of Rutgers' athletic history.

The team taught the university, the basketball community, and me a great deal. Rutgers won its first thirty-one games that year, was ranked fourth in the AP poll, and advanced to the 1976 NCAA Final Four. I had graduated but was still close to the coaches and players. I also was dating Jean.

Racial tensions were still present. I remember when Rutgers was recruiting a black player named James Bailey, a long-armed, high-jumping six-foot-nine center from Xaverian Brothers, a Catholic school outside Boston.

"I remember recruiting Bailey; it was a tense time in Boston when they were attempting to integrate the schools in South Boston and Charlestown," Rutgers assistant coach Joe Boylan remembers. "They lived in a walk-up in Roxbury, and I remember leaving the home one night and his dad—who was a big guy—said to me, "Now, if your car breaks down, you know you're white—you don't want to be walking around the streets here. You find a telephone and call me. We'll get you home safely."

"That attitude was prevalent throughout the team. The players always cared about one another. We were recruiting two kids from New England that summer. The other one was Mark Young, a six-foot-ten kid whose dad was a Naval officer stationed up there. I'd heard about them both from the late Don Slaven, a high school coach from Needham High School in Massachusetts who was inducted into the Massachusetts Coaches Hall of Fame. I loved Mark."

Joe goes on: "Don says, 'Do you know about Bailey?' I had read an HSBI [High School Basketball Insider] report from Five-Star founder Howard Garfinkel, who was not as enthusiastic. Don says, 'Joe, sometimes you need to watch the movie and not just read the review. The kid is a great kid, and he's going to be a great player.'" Turns out Bailey was talented. He could run, jump, and score.

"Rutgers lost Mark Young to Fairfield University but signed James and Abdel Anderson, a sleek six-foot-seven forward from Belleville, New Jersey, who turned out to be a three-year starter from 1977 to 1979 and a double-figure scorer who played in two NCAA tournaments and two NITs. In 1976, the coaches replaced Michael MacDonald and Lumpy Allen, a walk-on, on the roster. It was a heck of a tradeoff. James needed a summer job in Boston before he enrolled. He was a worker and through the Rutgers network was able to get a job in a huge factory."

"James was kind of shy, and the factory, like Xaverian Brothers High School, was not diverse," Joe recalls. "Like everything he ever did, he jumped in with both feet. I was not sure whether a black basketball player from a college prep school would fit in on the assembly line with people he never met. A week later, I figured I would check. I walked in, and the owner has this big smile on his face.

"The owner says, 'Come here. I want to show you something. I want you to look down and see who is sitting in the middle of all these guys at lunch.' It was James. They loved him. He could fix anything. I knew he would be a great attribute to our team and the Rutgers student body."

James Bailey earned the starting nod five games into the season. He was the final piece of the puzzle. He gave the team a shot blocker, which allowed wing players like Phil and Dabney to use their athleticism to jump the passing lanes and generate transition baskets. Ten years later, Texas Western University won the NCAA tournament; it was also the first time that Rutgers, a state university in the Northeast corridor with a diverse enrollment, started five black players. "We were putting the five best players on the floor," Tom Young recalls.

Though it was never said, it was more of a coincidence that both Don Haskins, head coach of Texas Western University, and Tom Young, head coach of Rutgers University, were both second cousins in the Hank Iba basketball family.

I was working for Jim Valvano, another Rutgers graduate, as he began his ascent in the college basketball ranks at Iona. I was scouting all upcoming opponents, but I did get to see Rutgers three times during the regular season. The team featured five future NBA players—Phil Sellers, Mike Dabney, Eddie Jordan, Hollis Copeland, and James Bailey, who gave Rutgers the inside presence it was looking for to compete nationally,

It was an express bus going straight to the Final Four.

The Scarlet Knights left the starting gates quicker than Secretariat at Belmont Park and just took off. And this was during an era with no three-pointer, no shot clock, and an NCAA ban on dunking until the following season. That team changed the way coaches thought the game could be played. Rutgers scored ninety points or more twenty-five times, including one hundred or more eleven times. And the games weren't close.

"We challenged ourselves in different ways during the games," Eddie recalls. "We wanted to see how high we could get our elbows over the rim."

Everyone loved it. Students would camp out overnight for tickets long before it was fashionable with Duke's Krzyzewskiville. Those who couldn't get in would watch the home games on closed-circuit TV from the gym annex. I don't think any of us bought a beer that season.

Rutgers began to draw national attention early in the season with a huge win against Boston College. That made Mark Conlin happy. When he signed at Rutgers after being snubbed by Boston College, the only thing he wanted to know was whether we had BC on the schedule. "After we crushed them 105 to 82 in Chestnut Hill, the coaches came up to congratulate me, and I told them what I thought of them," Mark recalls.

The Knights earned much deserved national attention after they blew by Penn, 95–80, at Madison Square Garden. Chuck Daly—who later coached the Detroit Pistons to two NBA titles and also coached the 1992 Olympics "Dream Team"—was Penn's coach at the time. He made this startling prediction about Rutgers: "I think that team can go unbeaten," he said after the game.

Tom let us enjoy the moment and be typical college students. There was a general understanding that there was a lot on the line. The players realized they needed to focus to be successful.

It didn't take long for the bandwagon to get crowded, and it became harder to contact Jean, as the phone lines were always busy in the basketball office.

"I used to sneak my friends in through the back door," Phil says. "When they would ask me where they were going to sit, I'd tell them, 'You're on your own.'"

The excitement carried over into the New York and New Jersey media. "It seemed like there were always people coming and going in the office," Jean says. "Reporters and TV crews were everywhere. They wanted to know everything about the players and coaches."

Phil Sellers was a two-time All-American who won the Haggerty Award as the best player in the New York metropolitan area. He was college basketball's version of Reggie Jackson, and he earned the nickname "Phil the Thrill" courtesy of Rutgers class of 1958 graduate Jose Carballal, who would become my future teammate at Xerox. Jose was a national account manager who had serviced Rutgers for thirty-four years. He was a huge Rutgers supporter and season ticket holder who made a

T-shirt for his young son, Joey, to wear to home games. "We had two tickets, and I used to alternate taking my son and daughter to the games," Jose recalls. "So, Joey and my wife, Rosalee, were home listening to the game on the radio, and he says to my wife, 'How come Phil doesn't have a nickname like "Earl the Pearl"?'

"We went to the bookstore and had a shirt made with 'Phil the Thrill' on it, and Joey started wearing it to the games. One night, Bob Smith, one of the sports information directors at Rutgers, grabbed Joey and Phil and put a picture of them in the alumni magazine, and it blew up from there. Suddenly, Joey was on the ten o'clock news on channel five in New York. The team adopted Joe, with Hollis Copeland and Sellers inviting him into the locker room to help with his homework before and after games. In turn, Joe felt like a good luck charm. 'If I wasn't there,' he said, 'I was letting the team down.'"

It was lucky for him, but unfortunately for his sister, she had to read about the games in the paper because tickets were at a premium.

Our teams were a happy, hardworking cast of characters. They embodied the funky 1970s with their Afros, long sideburns, and beards roaring down the court at a hundred miles per hour. All our players, like Phil, had nicknames. Eddie Jordan was "Fast Eddie." James was "Jammin' James," and Mike Dabney was "Dip." When I played, they used to call me "Ronald," after the character in the McDonald's commercial. Jeff Kleinbaum, a senior backup guard, became known as "Mr. One Hundred" because he scored the one hundredth point seven times.

It looked like there was no stopping this team after they buried Seton Hall, 119–93, at home just before Christmas. The Seton Hall Pirates had a good team that year with three of the team's all-time greats—Glenn Mosley, Greg Tynes, and Nick Galis. But Rutgers simply overwhelmed them. They say the Barn shook so hard that paint chips came floating down from the ceiling, caused by the tremendous vibrating noise and heat generated in the building, which forced a stoppage in play. Seton Hall was just a few exits away on the parkway, and we were saying, "We can't lose to them, because we'll never hear the end of it."

The Rutgers players knew their roles and were willing to accept them. With so many future pros, it could have been a problem. Dabney was a silky-smooth guard who had led East Orange High School to a Group III state championship and played for the legendary Roy Lester. He was willing to take a second seat to Phil and accept the fact that Eddie was just as important. He never got the attention those two did, but he always showed up. He finished second on the team in scoring, getting most of his points off steals and breakaways. And he was willing to adjust. Before Eddie came in, the other guards would throw the ball only to Phil or Dabney. But Eddie could do more things.

Mike Dabny, to his credit, was all about winning.

His basketball genes carried over to Maya Moore, his daughter, who became an All-American and a Wooden Award winner at the University of Connecticut, where she won two national championships. She also played for the U.S. national team, which won two gold medals in the 2012 and 2016 Olympics. Moore was a perennial WNBA all-star who left the league in 2019 to focus on criminal justice reform.

Rutgers had a couple of close calls during the streak. In early February, Eddie sprained his knee during a blowout of Delaware. The trainer told him to rest and keep it elevated. Eddie spent the next three days in his dorm room. He missed practice and no one could find him, because there was only one phone in the building, and it was down on the first floor. When the coaches finally tracked him down, Tom Young benched him for the next game against Manhattan. But when the Knights ran into foul trouble, Tom relented, putting him in during the second half, and Rutgers squeezed out a 92–81 victory in overtime.

Rutgers needed all the help it could get in its final game of the regular season. The team was leading against Saint Bonaventure 82–80 when Jim Baron stole the ball from Dabney on the open floor with thirty seconds left. Baron took two dribbles and then the whistle blew. A foul was called on Baron, and Dabney made both free throws, sealing an 84–80 victory. Rutgers finished the regular season 26–0.

There was pandemonium in the Barn that spilled out onto College Avenue. The team and its good luck charm, Joey, celebrated on the bus as they as they rode up College Avenue to Old Queens to ring the victory bell in the steeple to celebrate an unbeaten season.

"There must have been ten thousand people outside the Barn during the game," Jose says. "We're in this crowd and we can't find Joey. We decided to go back to the car, because we figured Joey would find us. He's standing next to our car with Phil, who made sure he got to me safely. Phil and Hollis took him everywhere. Hollis would even check his homework. That's just the type of guys they were."

Phil was the savior of Rutgers basketball.

"My freshman year at Rutgers in 1955, we were two and twenty-two," Jose recalls. "And the two teams we beat were Montclair State and Glassboro. My junior year, I was a cheerleader and we would go to games in the Barn and the place would be empty. It was bad. We recruited one kid when I was in school. He was six foot four and we thought it was a miracle we got a big guy. We had four hundred kids in my graduating class. We were like Lafayette, Lehigh. We were in that league."

Times changed during the Phil Sellers era. He had a pocketful of miracles. Fans were climbing through the windows to get into the Barn, and Rutgers was playing before big crowds in big games at the Garden. The biggest occurred when Rutgers played Saint John's again for the ECAC South championship and an automatic bid to the NCAA tournament before a sellout crowd.

Phil and Beaver Smith of Saint John's in Queens were involved in a classic struggle between two former New York City playground legends. Saint John's had a four-point lead with three minutes to play when Tom Young called a timeout. "Phil says, 'Hey, coach, give me the ball,'" Tom recalls. "I said, 'Phil, relax. We're going to do what we always do.' I started to draw up a play, and he repeats it. And I said the same thing. And then he repeats it a third time."

Tom could have ignored the request. "I was shocked when he said, 'Okay, give it to Phil,'" Phil says. He responded by scoring three straight times on Beaver Smith, and Rutgers won, 70–67, to earn an automatic bid to the NCAA tournament.

"He was toast," Phil says, chuckling. "He was burnt before we started cooking."

Rutgers' journey to the Final Four almost ended before it began. Their first game was against rival Princeton, the Ivy League champion.

The game was close.

Rutgers was clinging to a 54–53 lead with four seconds left when Peter Molloy, one of Princeton's guards, was fouled by Eddie Jordan far from the basketball. Molloy was a 90 percent free throw shooter, and he was awarded a one-and-one.

Tom Young called two straight timeouts to ice the shooter.

"I knew if we lost that game, we were going to be a flash in the pan," Hollis remembers. "Dabney said to me, 'Don't sweat it. This guy looks uneasy. He's going to blow it.'"

That's exactly what happened. Molloy's first attempt bounced off the iron, and Dabney—who was assigned with boxing out the shooter—flew in to grab the rebound as time ran out. "We had guardian angels on our shoulders that night," Phil says.

Those angels must have gotten an extended stay for one more weekend, helping to guide the team to the Final Four. Rutgers caught a break even before the tournament began when North Carolina was upset by Virginia in the ACC tournament and then promptly lost to DePaul University. The Scarlet Knights cruised through a weaker bracket in the East Regional Tournament in Greensboro, North Carolina, defeating Yankee Conference champion Connecticut University in the semifinals, then outscoring Virginia Military Institute, which upset DePaul, coached by future Naismith Hall of Famer Ray Meyer, 91–75, in the finals to advance to the Final Four in Philadelphia.

Because Rutgers was located just an hour away from Philly, and most of the team was from New Jersey or New York City, everyone on the team was besieged by family and friends for tickets. Practices were filled with pro scouts from the NBA and ABA, and agents were approaching the players. Rutgers got to experience the magnitude of the event when ten thousand fans showed up at a Friday afternoon practice at the Spectrum.

Rutgers was one of two undefeated teams left in the bracket, along with Indiana.

Joe Boylan made a point of introducing himself to iconic former UCLA coach John Wooden, who had retired the previous year after coaching his team to ten national championships. "Son," Wooden told him, "make sure you go out there and take a minute to look around at the crowd and take it all in. You never know when you are going to be there again."

He was right.

The magic dust settled on the floor of the Spectrum the next afternoon when the Scarlet Knights experienced the agony of their first defeat. They lost their first game of the year to Michigan, coached by the legendary Johnny Orr, 86–70. That team had future NBA players Phil Hubbard and Rickey Green. "It was really the worst feeling," Young said. "Your whole career you spend trying to get to that moment, and you have the worst shooting night of your life—in a game you should have won. We got good shots. We just couldn't throw it in the ocean."

The pain continued that Monday when Rutgers lost to UCLA by fourteen points in the consolation game.

The real disappointment was that Rutgers had played so much better during the year, winning thirty-one straight games.

Those wins were the result of many people's hard work, and unfortunately their success has been only a memory for Rutgers fans. It's a constant reminder to me that you are only as good as your next day at work.

It's funny. Years later, Eddie Jordan, who spent years as a player in the NBA and was the head coach of the Washington Wizards, invited me to watch a playoff game in D.C. Tom Young was there too, helping Eddie out. After the Wizards won, I walked into the locker room and saw Phil Hubbard, who had played on that Michigan team and was one of Eddie's assistant coaches. Eddie introduced me, and the first words out of his mouth were, "Are you one of the guys we played against in the Final Four when we beat your butt?" I started laughing. "No, Phil," I said. "I was at the national coaches' convention with my boss, Jimmy Valvano, and I was in the stands, trying to enjoy the game instead of scouting."

Memories.

The 1976 team was as much mine as theirs. Rutgers didn't have the best facilities or play in the biggest league. The team was not as celebrated as UCLA's or Kentucky's, but it was a group of special players with coaches who challenged them to be the best they could. The reason they were successful was that everyone from the administration on down allowed people to do their jobs well, and that's something I've learned: You don't have to look like everybody else or follow everyone who is successful. To paraphrase Frank Sinatra, they did it their way.

It was a good lesson for me later in life. I've realized that the reason I've been successful in business is that I and my team never worried about the competition. We were just concerned about being the best we could be.

That team will always be the gold standard for Rutgers basketball. It will always be beloved, because those guys won thirty-one straight games and they were good guys whom the alumni loved. Even though Eddie Jordan, who came back to coach the team in 2013, was struggling, the fans at the RAC (Rutgers Athletic Center) still loved Eddie as a person.

Rutgers had it going in those days. Everybody wanted to play that team. Jerry Tarkanian, the coach of UNLV's Running Rebels who went to the Final Four in 1977, agreed to play Rutgers at the Philadelphia Spectrum.

The team moved from the Barn to a new eight-thousand-seat arena across the river and went to postseason for the next three years, first as an independent team and then as a member of the Eastern Eight, which included Pitt, Villanova, and Penn State.

They created some waves in 1978 when they defeated Indiana State and Larry Bird, 57–56, before a standing-room-only crowd of 8,700 in the second round of the NIT at the RAC. James Bailey, who had been in foul trouble most of the game, stole an inbounds pass when Rutgers was trailing and, after a timeout, Rodney Duncan got the ball to him for a game-winning fifteen-foot jumper. Indiana State had the last shot of the game, but Bird was occupied by Rutgers' box-and-one defense, and his teammate Harry Morgan missed just before the buzzer. The postgame was wild, and Bird leveled a Rutgers fan who had jumped on his back in a melee; the guy ended up on his back with a bloody nose.

The Scarlet Knights had a shot to make a return trip to the Final Four in 1979 when they played Saint John's in the East Regional semifinals at Greensboro. "We had beaten Saint John's twice during the regular season, and I felt if we won that game we could have been Penn and gone to Salt Lake City the same year Magic and Bird were there," Tom says. "But it's hard to beat the same team three times in a season."

It was a heartbreaking loss. Rutgers had an eight-point lead in the second half but let it slip away, and big Wayne McKoy scored on a tip-in at the buzzer to give the Johnnies a 67–65 victory.

The RAC had and still has one of the greatest home court advantages in Eastern basketball, and Rutgers had a chance to keep the momentum going.

"Rutgers is located between Philadelphia and New York City, and North and South Jersey had tons of players," former assistant John McFadden says. "If you signed three of the top five prospects from Jersey, you were going to be a Top Twenty program every year." The Big East had a TV contract with ESPN. They were one of the first to have a postseason tournament. They were getting everybody. It was the red velvet rope everyone wanted to get behind.

The last time Rutgers won a game in the NCAA tournament was in 1983. Tom Young eventually headed south, leaving for Old Dominion in 1985. And before the 2020 season, the team had not been invited to the expanded NCAA tournament since 1991, though the Scarlet Knights seem to be going upstream under new coach Steve Pikiell, who had them poised to make the tournament in the coronavirus 2020 season. College basketball is all about the here and now, not about memories. "'Phil the Thrill' hasn't played for Rutgers in forty years," McFadden says. "They haven't had a lottery pick since James Bailey went sixth in 1979, or a first-round pick since James Hinson in 1983 and Quincy Douby in 2006."

But the 1976 team will always be beloved. And the school has taken every opportunity to reminisce and celebrate those players with reunions when fans could welcome them back at a home game every five years. The team represents what good leaders like Tom Young and team members who worked hard and took chances could accomplish, and it allowed everyone to enjoy little successes along the way. I tried to model that attitude every day in my own career.

CHAPTER 6

Looking for a Mentor

When I graduated from Rutgers, I was deciding whether to go into coaching or apply to law school. Our athletic director, Fred Gruninger, even wrote me a letter of recommendation when I applied to Duke.

Jim Valvano, another Rutgers graduate who was coaching at Bucknell at the time, made up my mind for me.

That summer, I spent two weeks working as a counselor at his summer basketball camp. I laughed the entire time. Jim must have seen me when I was working with the kids, because he called me up one day and asked if I would be interested in getting my master's degree at Bucknell as his graduate assistant.

I told him, "Jim, I'll go, I'll go."

It was a welcome suggestion, as I knew more coaches than lawyers, so I thought it would be more familiar. This was another time I didn't know what I didn't know.

Then the next day, Jim called back. Change of plans. "Mike, I just took the Iona job," he said. "The only thing they have is a business school. You all right going to business school? I thought you wanted to earn a master's degree in history?"

Well, what the heck. We really got along, and I knew from my experience it would be a fun ride. Besides, I enjoyed coaching kids, provided they bought into what I was saying. There were some kids who went to camp because their parents just wanted to get rid of them. They were the ones who had copies of *Playboy* magazine under their bunks. But the kids who wanted to learn basketball, they were a pleasure.

Little did I know it was going to be unlike any experience in my life at that point. Every day working for Jim came with its own thrills.

I know it made one person happy. When I had signed with Rutgers, Father Melton joked with me, "You know, Mike, you are going to an atheist school." Then I saw him again after I had signed on to coach at Iona College. "Nice to see you are back in the fold," he told me.

Jim was a man for all seasons. He could be tough when he needed to be. But he also made basketball fun, and he never lost sight of the fact that basketball was a game. When he would come to practice, he would have his warm-up suit on and he'd be clowning around with the kids, playing them one-on-one. Then he would put on a show at the games, getting tough on the officials when he disagreed with their calls. He was so funny that he never got the credit he deserved as a coach. I thought he was a great coach and a serious student of the game. If we lost, he'd stay up all night watching tapes and talking about what we could have done better.

If we won, it was pizza for everybody.

I got to know Jim in college because he was best friends with loyal Rutgers alum Abe Suydam. Abe used to invite me to dinner whenever Jimmy was in town. Abe's daughter Robin went to Bucknell when Jim coached there, and Abe got to know Jim and Bob Lloyd when they played in the same backcourt for his beloved Rutgers. Bob was one of seven consensus first-team All-Americans in 1967, along with future Hall of Famers Lew Alcindor (later Kareem Abdul-Jabbar) of UCLA, Elvin Hayes of Houston, and Wes Unseld of Louisville. Jim was the often-forgotten other guard on the NIT team that season.

But both were headed for bigger and better things. Bob became a multimillionaire in the software business and lived in Hawaii. Jim went on to coach the Wolfpack team at North Carolina State to an unexpected national championship win over heavily favored Houston in 1983. In that game, Lorenzo Charles scored on a follow-up at the buzzer, and Jim was seen running around the court at the Pit arena in Albuquerque, New Mexico, looking for someone to hug.

He had this to say to all those nonbelievers in the media:

"My favorite quote was, 'Trees would tap dance, elephants would drive the Indianapolis 500, and Orson Welles would skip breakfast, lunch, and dinner before NC State figured out a way to win the NCAA tournament,'" Jim says. "This team taught me that elephants are going to be driving in the Indianapolis 500 someday."

Jim became one of the first college coaches who used basketball as a springboard to financial success. He was an American original, the king of the one-liner. He used the Wolfpack's championship run to promote himself and NC State on the national stage. In the weeks following the championship, he made two trips to the White House to meet with President Ronald Reagan. The players were not allowed to go with him on the first trip because of an NCAA rule that prevented teams from traveling more than one hundred miles away from campus for a championship celebration. While Jim sat in the Oval Office with North Carolina senators Jesse Helms and John East, the players were hooked up to the White House by satellite from Raleigh TV station WRAL. On a second trip, Jim took two team members, Sidney Lowe and Dereck Whittenburg, with him.

In the months following the season, Jim entertained members of the media from all over the country who wanted to find out the secret of his success. He wrote a book chronicling his team's unexpected journey through March Madness and introduced his own clothing line, called Jimmy V. He also accepted a handful of endorsements, one for Mountain Dew soft drink and another from the Hardees food chain.

"I would like to think this is what my grandfather had in mind when he landed at Ellis Island from Naples, Italy," he says today. "I am what this country is supposed to be about. I don't have many hobbies. I don't play golf. I love traveling the country and taking the pulse of American business. All the things I did helped me promote my program and NC State and helped me do my job, which is to recruit the best student athletes I can so I can have the best basketball program."

Jim did as many as 150 personal appearances a year and raised his fee for corporate speeches with the Washington Speakers Bureau to fifty thousand dollars apiece as he began making weekly appearances on the CBS morning show with Phyllis George, a former Miss America. He was even offered his own TV talk show, with Vanna White as his sidekick, when he was being romanced by UCLA in the late 1980s.

"It was a whole new world for Jim," says Nick Valvano, one of Jim's brothers. "He wanted to do everything. He formed his own production company, JTV Enterprises. He became a fixture on the motivational speech circuit. His clothing line included a terry cloth wrap that basketball players could wear in the locker rooms that were being increasingly populated by female reporters. He commissioned an artist to do a signed print every year for the team that won the championship."

By 1985, Jim was the nation's highest-paid college coach, making nearly five hundred thousand dollars in salary and endorsements. "He was really too smart to be a coach," Dereck Whittenburg says. "He should have been on Wall Street."

I worked for Jim at his summer camps throughout my college career, and he was still polishing his act then. I got to know the entire Valvano family—his wife, Pam; his brothers, Nick and Bobby. Jim discovered what I knew about basketball and felt that I might make a good coach someday.

Jim was a character. He was the middle child of Rocco and Angela Valvano and grew up under the El tracks in Queens. His father coached basketball for thirty years at Saint Nicholas of Tolentine in the Bronx. Jim was a super outgoing kid. And he was always funny. He once said, "My mother said I was vaccinated with a Victrola phonograph needle. I haven't shut up since."

Jim attended the local parish school. "When he was six years old, the kids in school started giving him a hard time because he had a big nose in third grade," Nick recalls. "Jim started doing impressions of the famous comedian Jimmy Durante, who always joked he had a big nose. He was so good at it, the nuns used to parade him from classroom to classroom so he could do the bit. I guess you could say the nuns were Jimmy's first comic enablers."

The family eventually moved to Long Island, and Jimmy was a three-sport star at Seaford High School. The Kansas City Royals and San Francisco Giants both wanted to draft him in baseball, but his family insisted he go to college. Jim wanted to play basketball, but he was only six feet tall and 155 pounds, and recruiters weren't exactly beating down his door. He wanted to play for Saint John's, but the staff didn't think he was good enough.

He went to Rutgers without a scholarship, but he became a three-year starter and had a big moment at the Garden as a senior when he made nine straight shots and scored twenty-one points in the first half of a loss to eventual NIT champion Southern Illinois and Walt Frazier. He majored in English, but he wanted to follow in his father's footsteps and become a high school coach.

He married his high school sweetheart, Pam Levine. Then Bill Foster hired him to coach the Rutgers freshman team.

Jim loved the great Green Bay Packers' coach Vince Lombardi, and once told a story about how he planned to use one of Lombardi's inspirational pep talks on his Rutgers team prior to his first game as their coach. He planned to duplicate Lombardi by waiting three minutes before the team was supposed to take the court, then walking in and ripping open the door to the locker room, pointing to the tunnel, and telling his team they would be successful if they devoted themselves to three things: "First your family. Second, your religion. And third, Rutgers basketball." When Lombardi had said that, saying "Green Bay Packers" instead of "Rutgers basketball," of course, his team had raced through the door and won the game.

But instead, when Jim went to the door to open it, he fell on his face. When he got up, he turned to the players and said, "We will be successful if you devote yourselves to three things. First, your family, Second, your religion. And third...the Green Bay Packers."

Whoops.

Jim stayed at Rutgers for two years before getting his first head coaching job at Johns Hopkins in 1970. While he was at that elite academic school in Baltimore, Maryland, he also had duties as the ticket manager and the assistant lacrosse coach for a nationally ranked team even though I don't think he had ever even picked up a stick. In his only year with Johns Hopkins' Division III Blue Jays, he coached his team to a 10–9 record and made the NCAA tournament. He was as excited as can be, and he once shared that memory with me.

"Mike," he told me, "I'm excited. I'm thinking about my Rutgers team that went to the 1967 NIT and won a game. And one of the guys comes up and says, 'Coach, would you mind if I bring my girlfriend on the bus?' I didn't let him. Then I got everybody on the bus, and I look back and they are all reading books. I said to myself, 'Not one of us would be reading a book on the way to a game.' I didn't realize I had twelve future surgeons on board. These guys, they enjoyed playing basketball, but they were more concerned about getting into med school."

Then he said to me, "By the way, Mike, after they graduated, I could have had any doctor on our team treat me."

Jim was so funny that people tended to overlook how smart, intellectual, and well-read he was and how good he was as a young coach. When he coached Bucknell, he developed a reputation for using unconventional methods. For example, his on-campus radio show began with the theme from *The Godfather*. And during pregame warm-ups, he could be found in uniform, taking part in layup drills.

But you could see he had a future when he brought his team with guard Greg Purnell to a game at Rutgers in 1974. They were a .500 team, meaning they had the same number of wins as losses, but he stayed competitive in the first half of that game. And we had way better players.

When Jim took a coaching job at Iona in the spring of 1975, the team was coming off a dreadful 4–19 season and had only one player—Kevin Bass—who was good enough to earn minutes on our Rutgers team. But even though it was a small Catholic commuter school just outside New York City, that didn't stop Jim from dreaming big.

He was the best salesman ever. He could sell you anything. In a two-night period, he talked me out of going to Bucknell, where I was going to get a master's degree in liberal arts, and into going to business school at

Iona. Once I got there, he was already talking about how the team would win the National Championship some day and become a fixture on the back page of the *Daily News* sports section.

Jim taught me that basketball was a business. It was more than just setting picks and boxing out.

I learned how to sell the dream working for Jim.

When I made the transition to coaching, I also quickly learned that there wasn't really a playbook. There were plans, but you always had to be fluid, just as the game was. It was about adjusting on the fly if the first option didn't work. For example, if a good player breaks his leg, then you've got to make an adjustment. A kid might not have good grades, then suddenly he's ineligible to play. Stuff happens. You need to have an alternative strategy. If there is a problem, you need to know what to do next and come up with the best strategy going forward. You are constantly learning every day, and you can't lose that passion if you want to be successful.

It's the same in business.

Jim was an extrovert. He had the personality to be a star. I was more reserved at that point in my life. I worked for him for two years, and it was like being in a writers' workshop with Carl Reiner or Norman Lear. Johnny Carson was probably lucky that the metropolitan coaches' luncheons were held at Mamma Leone's in the city instead of near his studio in Burbank, California. Jim owned the room. He always spoke last because nobody, including Lou Carnesecca of Saint John's, wanted to follow his act. He'd do twenty minutes of stand-up comedy, then throw in a few lines about the team. The writers loved him.

Iona was located just beyond the Metro North train stop on North Avenue. It looked nice. It was a pretty, tree-lined campus located near one of the best neighborhoods in New Rochelle, New York. When I arrived, I asked Jim where I would live. He told me Iona had only one dorm with 320 rooms for undergraduates. He told me the only room available was in the power plant. I was in the same building as the plumbers, electricians, and building managers. I felt at home. I felt like I was at my childhood home on Park Avenue, though I didn't have a union card. So, I'd be taking a shower in the morning and a plumber would walk in. It was not the tree-lined street that Kris Kringle promised Natalie Wood in *Miracle on 34th Street*. My room would never be mistaken for a suite at the Plaza.

As a result, Jean would never visit. I spent as much time on the Jersey Turnpike traveling to visit her as I did scouting and recruiting promising high school prospects to Iona. I followed Jim's lead and learned to network, which resulted in the maintenance crew's offering me a summer job.

I needed to make some extra cash. My stipend included tuition, room, and meals. I was on my own for books. I would work for Jim all day, then go to class at night. But the time spent with Jim and the skills I learned from him would pay dividends down the road and far outweighed the dollars I would have made working a regular job.

I spent a lot of my downtime at Jean's parents' house in South River, New Jersey, during those two years, including one Christmas. "Mike used to tell me how he never got many presents because he came from such a big family," Jean recalls of my childhood. "So, he wakes up and there's five boxes with his name on them. He was so excited. He was like a little six-year-old kid."

When I was working at Iona, my chief responsibilities were scouting the opposing team, helping assistant Tom Abatemarco with recruiting, and providing academic support for our players.

When Jim accepted the Iona job, it was late in the recruiting process. But like everything Jim did, he exceeded expectations. Through effort, performance, and true luck, he did a great job recruiting for the small commuter school, which had not yet established its traditions in New York City basketball. He went to New Jersey and signed Dave Brown, a six-foot-five forward from Essex Catholic High School to play with Kevin Bass. Dave scored over 1,500 points and grabbed over a thousand rebounds in his career, and Iona went from having four wins to being 10–16. We also signed Glenn Vickers and Kevin Hamilton, two great guards from Babylon and North Babylon high schools on Long Island, near his hometown.

Jim always had great success as a recruiter. He was relentless. He listened and he had the ability to make his visions everyone's reality. I was learning as much about business from him as I was in my night school classes. When I sat in his office when I arrived at Iona, he said to me, "Mike, we're going to win a national championship."

I said, "You mean here? With the Gaels? When I was at Rutgers, we had one thousand buildings. You're asking me to give recruits campus visits. It's going to take eighteen minutes."

Then he laid out his marketing strategy. "Mike," he said, "let me tell you something. Here's what the campus visit is going to look like. Say you're going to recruit Willie Sims from Long Island City. You're going to pick up Willie and you're going to take him downtown to Madison Square Garden. You're going to show him the Garden. Tell him, 'Willie, if you come to Iona, you're going to play X amount of games at the Garden.'

"Then you're going to walk over to Penn Plaza. Bill Maloney is a huge Iona alum. He runs the office products division for IBM. Take the elevator up to his office, and Bill is going to tell Willie he has a great chance to work as a summer intern for IBM. If he doesn't make it in the NBA, IBM is his future. Then, after Bill, ride around Manhattan, show him Central Park. That's probably three hours. Then you're going to take him to the College of New Rochelle."

"Why am I going to the College of New Rochelle?" I asked.

"That's the only place that has girls," Jim said. "So, I want you to take him there, get out of the car, walk around the campus, and have him feel like we will have a good social life. Then you can drive to Iona for the campus tour. That will take maybe fifteen minutes."

Here was the differentiating factor at Iona: Brother Driscoll, the school president, understood the value of athletics and would talk to every recruit.

Then each recruit would see Jim.

Jim was the greatest closer I ever saw.

If I got a recruit to Jim's office after I did all the things he told me to do, I was in good shape. The trip I thought would be fifteen minutes tops turned into a six-hour marketing event. Jim's whole deal was, "We're playing in New York. We're going to say that to any kid from New York City, the Island, Philadelphia, and Washington, D.C. They're going to play in the Garden, live in a beautiful place like Westchester County, and be close to the greatest city in the world."

We didn't get Willie. He went to Louisiana State University. I guess he wanted to be the next "Pistol Pete." But I said to myself, "We can recruit here. There's no doubt we can get players."

I remember we were visiting a recruit at home once. Jim talked so fast, and he introduced himself to the family like this: "Jim Valvano, Iona College."

The father was stunned. "If you own a college," he said, "maybe we can get a dorm."

And Jim could coach. He could take average talent and beat better teams. He had an ability to make his players relax in tough situations. My first year there, the team was young and still needed some improvement, but we upset Saint John's at home. Jim had those kids believing they were as good as any team in the city, including Saint John's, which was ranked in the AP Top Twenty. It must have been a shock to Louie (Lou Carnesecca, head basketball coach at Saint John's). Saint John's never scheduled us again.

During a game at Columbia in Jim's first season as coach, Iona rallied from being seventeen points down to finally winning in double overtime. Jim got so excited during the comeback that he keeled over at courtside, blacking out for a second.

Jim loved every sort of competition, including recruiting. He was just thirty-two years old, but he was far worldlier than me and thought he would recruit and coach the best players. And he could really teach the game. The players responded to him when they discovered how into it he was.

The second year, Jim went after the biggest star of them all: Jeff Ruland from Sachem High School North in Suffolk County, New York. Ruland was a six-foot-eleven, 280-pound center who was averaging twenty-eight points a game as a senior and was being recruited by Indiana, UCLA, Notre Dame, North Carolina, Wake Forest University, and us. Ruland thought he was the best player in the country, and he might have been right.

His mother, Anita, owned a bar on Long Island. We had a five-thousand-dollar recruiting budget, so all of the Iona coaches got in a car and drove out there and just sat with Mrs. Ruland at work, and Jim would share his vision of Jeff and Iona College. We must have ordered every item on the left and right side of the menu. Tommy Abatemarco, an assistant coach at Iona, who lived on the Island, used to stop at Ruland's home every day on his way to work and leave a note on the windshield of Ruland's car because he couldn't afford the toll on the Throgs Neck Bridge. We even made the decision to pull off the full-court press on two PSAL stars who would end up in the NBA—Rolando Blackman and Franklin Edwards—because Jim didn't want to recruit over Glenn Vickers and Kevin Hamilton. Jim felt Ruland would feel more comfortable playing with Glenn and Kevin.

Jim didn't miss a beat. We attended every one of Jeff Ruland's high school games. One night we were there, Joe B. Hall—the head basketball coach of the University of Kentucky—flew up on a private plane with some bankers from Lexington to watch him play.

"Hey, Jimmy," Hall said, "I hear you think you are going to get Ruland. He's being recruited by UCLA, North Carolina, and us. And you think you're going to get him?"

Then one of the bankers said, "I'll tell you what, Jim. You get him. We'll buy Iona and move that sucker to Kentucky."

I'm not sure whether Brother Driscoll ever got a call about selling Iona.

But Jim believed in himself and followed his plans. He wasn't intimidated by the names on people's jerseys, on the court or off it. He felt Jeff could be a game changer for the program, and he expected us to drive out to Lake Ronkonkoma and Sachem High School to be at his games. Once, when Jim had a conflict, he asked me to go to one of Jeff's games. I had a marketing exam that night with one of the many great professors at Iona. Jim told me not to worry about the exam. So, I went out to watch Jeff's game. When I got back, the professor failed me because I missed the exam.

This was a lesson learned. It was the first time I had ever left something to chance, something I would never do again. I was disappointed in myself. I realized it takes a lot of balancing to be successful in everything.

Failing that class was the only thing that prevented me from having an MBA.

The only thing that made it easier to digest was signing Jeff Ruland. In the end, it came down to the fact that Jeff's father had died when he was young, and he wanted his mother to watch him play. The drive to Iona was doable. Three years later, in 1980, Jim and Jeff put Iona on the map. Iona was 29–5 and was ranked nineteenth in the country when the team blew away the eventual national champion Louisville Cardinals by seventeen points at the Garden. The Cardinals were number one in the country at the time. The Iona Gaels made it to the NCAA tournament for a second consecutive season and advanced to the second round before losing to Georgetown University by three points.

I wasn't around to see those games, and it wasn't because my lease at the power plant had ended. I had decided to go into the real world. I had been coaching for a guy who was driven to succeed, and I was part of his success. But I had to make my own way. I didn't want to live in the boiler room all my life. I had to chart my own course.

In one of the classes I didn't miss, I met a number of IBM junior executives who were also getting a master's degree at night. As much as Jim taught me, these guys showed me how much I could make in sales.

One IBM account manager in his mid-thirties used to drive up to class in a BMW. He would have a great suit on. I had a budget deficit. This guy had a James Bond life to me.

For all my parents provided me, I also realized what we didn't have. I wanted to marry Jean, and coaches in that era didn't make that much money. A head coach made less than the average high school teacher, and the assistants always had two jobs.

I learned a lot that year. Most important, as much as I loved coaching basketball, I realized I was only as good as my next win. It was hard for me to imagine buying a house for a family on a coach's salary.

CHAPTER 7

Selling Yourself

When I realized the risks and rewards of coaching, I knew that I was comfortable with what I had done, no matter where I had been: growing up in Upper Darby, working summer camps, playing for Tom Young, working for Jim Valvano. I was confident in what I had learned and eager to take on new challenges.

At this crossroads in my life, I had three doors to choose from. Through networking, which is what every coach does, I interviewed with three Fortune 500 companies—Procter & Gamble, IBM, and Xerox. The many contacts I had made at Iona's Hagan School of Business allowed me to interview well with IBM in its office products division. Even though I was offered the job, there was a lack of connection between me and the IBM sales rep whom I traveled with. During my interview, he did not represent the company I had learned about and admired through friends. It was so bad, we went to lunch and I had trouble making conversation over a Nathan's hot dog.

I was also offered a job by Procter & Gamble in Connecticut, but it would have required me to sell Crisco oil. I didn't spend much time in the kitchen, and Crisco wasn't right for me.

With doors one and two closed, I realized, like every good salesman, that I had to keep knocking on doors.

Fortunately for me, Tony Olivo, who worked in the Rutgers alumni relations office, contacted another Rutgers alum, Jose Carballal, the huge Scarlet Knight basketball fan I told you about earlier. He worked for Xerox and was the national account manager for the state of New Jersey.

Xerox was setting new standards in business in 1977. It was a pioneer in office technology and the first corporation to manufacture imaging-process plain-paper copiers in 1959. Xerox expanded into other products and went on to develop word-processing machines in 1974; laser printers in 1977; Ethernet, an office communications network, in 1979; and eventually digital photocopiers.

Jose set me up for an interview with Barry Slaughter, one of the hiring managers in the Princeton office.

"We had hired a couple of former athletes from Rutgers, like football star J. J. Jennings, but not a lot," Jose recalls. "Tony called me up and said, 'Hey, I got this great kid, former basketball player. He's working for Jim Valvano up at Iona, and he wants to get into business.' But he told me he had given a commitment to Valvano to stay at Iona until April, when recruiting ended."

Jose talked to Barry, but Xerox is all about the process. Management wants all new employees to start in January.

Barry's initial response was no.

"I really liked Mike," Jose says about me. "So, I went to my boss, John Fillman, who was also Barry's boss. I pitched Mike to him. Fillman told me he would interview him and, if Mike was any good, he'd try to work something out.

"The funny thing was, I had to arrange the interview through Mike's fiancée, Jean, who was still working for Tom Young. She facilitated an interview at the basketball office at the Athletic Center. Mike was in his comfort zone and sold himself to Fillman, who assured him he would save a territory for him. But I was the one who had to tell him there were no sports jackets in the C-suite like there was on the sideline."

"He's got to wear a suit," Fillman said.

"I was excited and called Mike," Jose says. "I told him he's going to have a job, but then he told me he's getting married in May and going on a one-week honeymoon. Somehow it all worked out."

Though I had no idea how working for Xerox would impact my life and the lives of many others, I had a great feeling when I traveled with one of the sales reps. He treated me exceptionally well, was extremely professional, and appeared genuinely excited for me.

It's a good thing he didn't work as a recruiter for Kentucky. Jeff Ruland might have ended up there.

My first job with Xerox paid $14,400, and the start date was April 4, 1977. That was the start of spring recruiting for all college basketball. I felt good about leaving Jim at that point. I had kept my commitment, and the team was on to the next class. After Jean and I got married, we rented an apartment in East Brunswick, New Jersey.

Jim didn't understand the move. He was a basketball guy. I had been part of his team, and now he had to recruit another coach as well as a player. But I made the decision and never looked back. I did not want to put myself in a career where historically there was a ceiling on money. I also feared that to move up as a coach, I'd have to leave the East Coast. My wife was an only child, and I promised her I'd never move farther than six hours away from her parents. When we were in Rochester all those years, we could make the drive to Jersey in five and a half hours. Our new home was also close to my family in Upper Darby.

Though I was only twenty-three years old, I was focused on the potential that Xerox offered and knew what I wanted: to provide for my family and make the most of the opportunity.

This was a much different mindset than I had during my senior year at Rutgers. In basketball, you have limitations. You can only run so fast and jump so high, and I had maxed out as a shooter. But in business, you can achieve whatever you want if you put in the effort. There are no limitations. If you have the education, if you want to learn, if you can work with people on a team, you can achieve whatever you want.

I was as proud to earn my business card at Xerox as I was to earn my varsity jersey at Bonner. Xerox was very selective about whom it hired.

The whole family: (left to right) My son-in-law Anthony Cali, my daughter Stacey Cali, my granddaughter Cameron, myself, my grandson Christian, my wife Jean, my son Chris, my granddaughter Reese, my grandson Ryten, my daughter-in-law Lauren, my granddaughter Roree, my son Ryan, dog Bentley

My wife Jean and I

Jean's parents, Edward and Honora Murock

Mike's parents, Bradley and Florence MacDonald

Me, Mike Weir, and my brother Robert

My executive photo for Xerox

Playing basketball in the gym at Rutgers

Me with Dick Vitale

Me with Alan Greenspan, former chair of the U.S. Federal Reserve, and Tom Donohue, head of the U.S. Chamber of Commerce. I was on the board of the Chamber of Commerce at the time.

Phil Mickelson and I at the Phoenix Open, playing in the pro-am

Family reunion: (left to right) Me, my sister Florence, brother Brad, sister Margaret, and brother Robert

Fred Couples and I at the Phoenix Open

Tiger Woods and I at the 1999 Phoenix Open

THE 1974 - 1975 RUTGERS UNIVERSITY BASKETBALL TEAM (22 - 7)
FIRST EVER NCAA TOURNAMENT PARTICIPANT
RANKED 16th, IN COUNTRY BY A.P.--- ECAC METROPOLITAN CHAMPION
Kneeling (L.to R.) Jonas Ameer, Mgr., Stanford Nance, Mike MacDonald, Sylvester
Allen, Mark Conlin, Ed Jordon, and Jeff Kleinbaum.
Standing (L.to R.) Tom Young, head coach, Art Perry, JV coach, Mike Dabney,Bruce
Scherer, Les Cason, Mike Palko,Steve Hefele,Hollis Copeland,Phil Sellers,
Joe Boylan, Assistant coach, and John McFadden Assistant coach.

The 1975 Rutgers team, the first Rutgers team to go to the NCAA tournament

Dan Chard, Wayne Anderson, me, and Jason Groves

Me with former professional player for the Cincinnati Bengals and Rutgers All American Marco Battaglia

Head coach of Rutgers, Steve Pikiell, and I

Jason Groves and I at the Stock Exchange

Medifast team ringing the opening bell in March 2020

I remember when thirty graduates from colleges in Jersey were inter-viewing there. There were ten from Rider, ten from Princeton, ten from Rutgers. Though well-educated, some candidates didn't have the back-ground in math they needed to pass the basic test at Xerox. Although I had been a liberal arts major at Rutgers, my two years of graduate school had given me a good foundation in business. I also had been fairly good at counting other people's minutes at Rutgers and figuring out there wouldn't be too many left for me.

One of the first things that happened when I went to Xerox was that I, like everyone else, was invited by Howard Langan to a picnic in the park. He was the branch manager at the Princeton office. He was successful, quite a presence, and revered by everyone on the team.

I made it my goal that afternoon to be in his shoes in ten years, which I accomplished.

When I first went to Xerox, I admit it was a culture shock. I had no formal business experience. I had never worked as a summer intern. The only thing I had done was meet Bill Maloney, the big IBM guy who was an Iona supporter, when I was at graduate school there. That was my frame of reference. And I knew Abe Suydam, who owned his own business in New Jersey. But a large, buttoned-down corporation like Xerox was foreign to me. At Iona, we had worn leisure suits and patent leather shoes. Assistant coach Tom Abatemarco and I used to look like we were going out on Halloween.

I relied on the skills I had learned from my college basketball coaches and translated them into private business. I applied Bill Fos-ter's organizational skills as well as the ethics that he and Dick Lloyd had displayed when I worked for them at summer camps. I was com-fortable in leading a team using Tom Young's coaching style, which had created a winning program. I also had learned the importance of details and empathy from Joe Boylan. And at Xerox, I learned the ins and outs of my product the same way John McFadden knew his opponents after he scouted them. Though my sales approach was as enthusiastic as Dick Vitale's and Jim Valvano's, I'm certain I would have lost if we were recruiting the same player.

The long car rides with Jim and Dick allowed me to have great success in sales. I spent so much time around Jim; it was like a seminar in dealing with people. I had been quiet at Bonner and had become more outgoing at Rutgers. But Jim helped me learn that if you want to succeed, you need to put yourself out there and know your product better than anyone. And you need to take some risks. I was never afraid to cold-call people. I would walk into the office of a doctor or a lawyer, and I would look at their desk and see what they did. Did they play sports? Did they travel?

I walked into the Xerox office my first day wearing a lime green suit I had just bought at JCPenney that I thought was nice. As a blue-collar kid who had gone to Catholic school and always wore uniforms, I didn't have much experience buying clothes. The salesman at Penney must have seen me coming a mile away. I thought I looked good as I walked into the office and was introduced to Tom Zegarelli (aka "Ziggy"). He was one of Xerox's top sales reps in New Jersey, and he asked me what I was wearing.

Jose, my friend, thought the suit was going to start blinking and wondered if it needed batteries. I was naive enough to think I looked good, and I told him I bought two of them.

Ziggy said to me, "I'll tell you what. I want you to go home. Throw that suit out, and I want you to go buy a blue suit or a blue pinstripe suit, white shirts, maybe one blue shirt, and that's going to be your uniform for Xerox."

I never wore the brown suit I bought.

Later, Jose asked Ziggy what he thought.

"He's going to be good," Ziggy said. "But tell him to get rid of that freaking suit."

So basically, the first day I was there, I was thrown out of Xerox faster than Tom Young had thrown Phil Sellers out of practice. I knew I had to find the money to buy new suits.

I knew I had a lot to learn, but they never humiliated me. They cared for me because I was part of their team. They told me, "Hey, this is what it is and this is what you have to do." It was no big deal. They mentored me.

Ziggy called me on another day and shared with me what I needed to do to make sure I was successful. He said, "Look, you're new. I'm handling big accounts. You handle small accounts, so you learn sales."

He also told me about numbers. He said, "If you want to be successful in sales, you got to make a hundred calls a week. You got to go see twenty people a day. At the end of the week, you might come out of it with ten good prospects. After four weeks, you are going to get forty good prospects and seven or eight orders a month. That's what I want you to do."

He got me a planner and set me up. And I was willing to put in the time.

I went out and did what he had said. I made a hundred calls a week. In my first year at Xerox, I quadrupled my salary with commissions, and it allowed Jean and me to buy our first home, in South River, New Jersey.

Xerox's CEO at the time was David Kearns, who eventually became the deputy secretary of education for President George H. W. Bush. He was big on sales training. He was a legend in the company. He put tremendous emphasis on developing his employees' potential. He thought treating everybody equally was the right thing to do in a corporation. When I joined Xerox, we had a training center in Leesburg, Virginia, where employees went to study professional sales techniques before they could start on the sales force. When we went to the training center to learn about the Xerox 9400 duplicator, we had to memorize a twenty-five-page demonstration book. Anyone who did not hit one hundred key phrases during a demonstration got sent home. Over my thirty-three-year career, I must have spent a year in training courses.

One time, Xerox was getting into high-end printers and put me into what was known as the Astronaut program. I was in school for two and a half months. So, Xerox employees were always learning. I'm sure most people don't realize the work that goes into becoming successful.

Every employee was lucky that Xerox, like my parents, realized the importance of education, whether it was leadership or management training. The investment in people helped Xerox become one of the top companies in the world, but it created stiff competition to get promoted ahead of peers. It reinforced what Tom Young had showed the Scarlet

Knights about teams: that it took teammates playing many different types of roles to be successful.

Because I had played at Rutgers and worked in New Jersey, a lot of local businessmen knew who I was. I would drive down Route 27 in Edison, New Jersey, looking for any new business in my territory. There was a trailer on the side of the road. One day I walked in and saw Tony Yelencsics, a car dealer who was a big Democratic politician and who was running for mayor of Edison. He was a big fan of the Scarlet Knights and had good relationships with the coaches.

Anyway, Tony was using an old stencil machine to print out brochures. I said, "Tony, we have a device, the 660 copier, and you can use it to print out hundreds of copies in an hour. It costs two thousand two hundred dollars. You can use it for a couple days, and if you like it you can buy it and save yourself a few hundred dollars."

So, he used it and won the election, became mayor of Edison. The machine went to Boro Motors and wound up in the accounting office.

That sale was easy.

But sales in general are about rejection and persistence. I learned a lot about rejection from not making the team at Bonner, and from having to fight for playing time at Rutgers, where I was a three-star player playing with four- and five-star recruits. I was used to being in a role where I had to work harder and had to do more. At Xerox, I would make my twenty calls a day and get thrown out of fifteen offices. But I did well with the five or six I did get in with.

I sold a lot of machines based on where I had played basketball and what I was selling. I viewed myself as a representative of Rutgers and Xerox, so I had to make sure things were done the right way. I was constantly amazed by the number of Rutgers alums who wanted to help a graduate.

My success reinforced Ziggy's idea of showing up in person to your customers frequently. I was constantly on the phone setting appointments, then spent all day driving a stick-shift Ford Fairlane with no air conditioning from one customer to another.

I was selling the full line of copiers and eventually moved from small accounts to big accounts. I also sold Xerox Memorywriters. I was selling all our products at Rutgers. In addition, one of my first accounts was the *Asbury Park Press* newspaper. I sold to a lot to doctors and lawyers. And the selling was based primarily on personal relationships at the time. People were not buying from the superstores. I was developing long-term relationships with my clients. I was hitting all my bonuses.

The following year, 1979, Don West, my manager, came in and told me, "We're going to do a big reorganization. We're going to take you out of this territory and put you back into small accounts, because we want to prop up that area of the company."

In my previous job, I had been all but guaranteed a five-thousand-dollar bonus for the first two quarters. Now, that was up in the air. But I didn't complain. I realized playing basketball that you had to go where the team needed you. I went in to see the branch manager, Rich Barton, and I said, "Okay, if I do this and I perform, I'd like to be promoted to a high-volume sales representative with a pathway to management." It worked. I went to this low-volume job and I had the top numbers in the country. Xerox noticed and put me on a fast track. I was promoted after only one year to high-volume sales representative, selling higher-priced products. Just three years into my career at Xerox, I became one of the youngest sales managers in the history of the company. I was a twenty-six-year-old sales manager, responsible for a team on which many people were over forty. It was the ultimate player-coach experience. Ziggy used to call me "The Kid." Years later, when I was named president of North American Solutions, he sent me a note that said, "Congratulations, kid." I was fortunate it was a good territory. It included the state of New Jersey, including all of the schools, local governments, military, universities and colleges in a six-county area in central Jersey.

I was successful because I got my career off to a good start at Xerox, knowing what I didn't know and getting the best people to share their knowledge with me. And I wasn't afraid to listen. Mike Cardillo, who had played behind Jim Valvano at Rutgers, was a great sales manager and would run management training sessions. I would attend every session I could.

Though I probably would have thought differently on the playgrounds of Upper Darby, I learned that leadership skills can be developed. I was able to develop my own. Being a decent student and basketball player, I'd always enjoyed learning.

Working at Xerox provided me with the exposure to learn business and the mechanics of running an organization. Lifetime learning is an important aspect of being successful in business. Ziggy and Jose realized I was willing to learn; therefore, they gave me a chance.

They reinforced the idea of being enthusiastic and developing good work habits along with the technical aspects of business transactions. They also demonstrated the importance of working "smart"—how to do sales, how to prepare sales proposals, how to deal with customers.

It was challenging going from sales to management. Though I had always held teammates accountable, I had to become more effective. I had to become a better communicator so I could help people reach their goals while holding them responsible for their actions. I also learned that, as much as I supported everyone, if they couldn't be successful, then I had to fire them.

That was hard.

I realized early on that my providing a good example was the best way to hold people accountable. I guess it was a carryover from never blaming anyone for the shots I had missed or the mistakes I had made on the court. If I did not perform as a sales rep or manager, if I didn't work as hard as my team, the onus was on me. I made it a priority to always communicate my expectations and goals to everyone on my team. We all knew our roles. For me, it meant traveling with them and leading them in a way I thought they needed. I made the same personal investment in my team that they made in me. And it worked.

When the players push the coach, it really works. Seven people from my sales team eventually became vice presidents.

Sometimes it doesn't work. If individuals don't want to work or are not producing, then you need to address the problem. At Xerox, we called it corrective action. That meant in six months, nonperformers could be gone. In basketball, if a player doesn't perform, he goes to the bench, and eventually he's sitting in the stands instead of with the team on the floor. Basically, he gets cut.

I definitely needed to address things, managing a team on which all of my sales reps were older. When I fired the first guy for not carrying his weight, the older employees were like, "Holy geez, this kid is willing to step up to the plate." They weren't as complimentary when I stepped up and fired a guy who was considered their star first baseman. He was a guy who wanted to do things his way. One time I was meeting him at a diner for breakfast at eight o'clock in the morning. I got there, we had something to eat, and I was ready to go make calls because companies open at nine o'clock. And he was still sitting there, reading the New York *Daily News*. He was trying to send me a message: "I'm going to do things when I'm ready to do them and not be held to the team's schedule."

Well, six months later, that guy wasn't at Xerox anymore.

The point being, as much as I was willing to help people succeed, I wasn't afraid to address problems. The two things I always felt were important were holding people accountable and making tough decisions. One thing that separates an average executive from a good executive is not playing politics. Trying to be everybody's best friend doesn't always work. I always tried to get along with everybody, but no one was going to walk over me.

It was equally important to recognize people when they did a good job. Funny story. One time, in 1980, I was working for Rich Barton and I took my sales team to the Meadowlands raceway for lunch and the track to celebrate their performance. I was a young guy, and it was the day Phil Simms—a quarterback from Morehead State who was the first-round pick of the Giants—was being shown around, and we got a chance to meet him. I had no idea how expensive the Meadowlands was, so I got the bill for my eight sales reps and a couple of other guys, and it was like $1,800. I said to myself. "Holy cow, I'm going to have to pay for X amount of this out of my own pocket." We drove back, and the guys were excited.

I was dying because I had to tell Rich. I went back to his office and said, "You aren't going to believe what this cost."

He said to me, "Don't worry about it. You and your team are working hard. I'll take care of this." Even if Rich hadn't taken care of it, I would have paid my share, but I wouldn't have told Jean until a couple of months later.

When rewarding your team, I learned, it was always important to give of yourself. I was constantly telling workers if they were doing a great job, and I made sure to have luncheons, special events, Christmas parties at my house to make sure the people who worked for me felt good about it.

Tom Dolan was my branch manager for four years, from 1982 through 1986. He played a big role in helping me climb the corporate ladder. We had a lot in common. He had been a varsity track athlete at Manhattan College, and we became good friends. There was no way anyone could have realized his impact on Xerox. He was a mentor to me and the older brother of Anne Mulcahy, who became the CEO of Xerox in 2001.

Tom was the ultimate bootstrapper. He found his true calling in sales after spending two years in the Army after college.

"I was going to Brooklyn Law School, partially because I thought it was a good way to avoid the draft in the Vietnam era," he says. "After my second year there, I had just gotten married, came back from my classes, and found a draft notice in the mail. In 1968, they had dropped graduate school deferments. I went in as a sergeant in the infantry."

Tom was supposed to be shipped off to Vietnam, but at the eleventh hour, plans changed because his son was born with serious medical problems. He was encouraged to apply for compassionate reassignment, and he was assigned to Fort Dix in New Jersey. His first assignment was as a drill sergeant. It lasted two months before the post commander, looking for help in headquarters, read his profile and contacted him.

"Are you the guy who has a college degree with two years of law school?" he asked Tom. "What the hell are you doing down here?"

"Well," Tom told him, "it's two years instead of four, so that's one reason, and this is the assignment that I got."

Tom recalls, "Then he wanted to know if I could write and type. I went and started writing a lot of action plans and intelligence plans for him. While I was there, I met a guy, Bill McGuire, who was the Xerox sales rep at Fort Dix. We started talking, and he asked what I was going to do when I got out. I told him I'd like to go back and finish law school, but I didn't have the money because I was married with a child. I figured I'd work for a couple years, then go back and finish."

McGuire told Tom they were hiring at Xerox in Philadelphia, and he went in for an interview as soon as he was discharged. "I know they were impressed when I told them I had graduated from Chaminade, a good Catholic school on Long Island," he says. "The fact I also worked as a Good Humor ice cream man for six years because I wasn't on full scholarship showed them I knew how to sell.

"I got the job. That was better than the golden ticket from Willie Wonka.

"I figured I'd only stay for two years and get my law degree. Well, those two turned into thirty-nine, and I eventually became the president of global sales.

"Throughout most of my career, I loved being in the field and doing the work. When we were putting together big deals, I inserted myself into the transaction. I thrived on being part of the deal. In those days when Xerox won the Malcolm Baldrige National Quality Award presented by the National Institute of Standards and Technology, I was selected to represent the company. I spoke to other company CEOs and corporate senior executives about how we maintained our quality.

"It's funny. For me, I was lucky. At Xerox, the processes made us successful. I lived my life the same way. I can honestly say I never minded the work. Any successful senior executive lives with their team and their clients. That's not possible if you lead from behind. Mike was successful for the same reasons," he says of me. "That's why I trusted him. That is why he moved ahead at Xerox. A lot of these jobs were not cushy positions. But Mike and I worked hard, led by example, and were able to stick around for a long time. Like Mike, I led by example. Everyone knew we were on the same team.

"I attempted to be part of a team, rather than being removed. There are too many executives who choose to delegate everything to their people. You can't just delegate and keep your head in the clouds. My success came from getting down in the trenches and learning what was going on in their world. I realized I could find out more about organizations by traveling with sales reps one day a month. When I was running a large organization, I could find out whether our programs were working or not, what sort of issues were out there, and it was a way to stay connected.

"I saw Mike's production and knew he was a high performer. When I first met him, I'm guessing he was thirty. But he stood out from the other managers because of his maturity. He values employees on his team. You wouldn't find Mike in the office too often. That doesn't mean he was on the golf course. In the end, it was reflected in his team's work. They were always top in our region. It led to Mike being promoted to the manager of our Oradell facility, which was a much larger organization.

"Mike was always a competitive guy. I think it goes back to being an athlete. More important than that, Mike did not want to lose; he really wanted to win. He also shared the credit with his entire team. He made people feel special, and as a result they trusted him.

"We got to know each other professionally and personally. After work, we'd occasionally go out for a couple of beers and talk about sports and what they meant in our lives. Mike, who was the father of three young children, would eventually start looking at his watch because he wanted to get home to Jean and his kids. It showed he had balance in his life, which would serve him well as he received more responsibility in the company."

CHAPTER 8

The Journey

When I first started working at Xerox, I became successful at selling because it was similar to recruiting with one of the best recruiters ever, Jim Valvano. Though I never completed my master's degree at Iona, I will always be grateful for the "doctorate" in personal selling he provided me.

In addition to the great training at Xerox, I was fortunate to learn the importance of building a team. One thing I still needed in my professional career was a mentor. I found all that and more in Ed Ciaschi.

Ed has been a close friend and trusted advisor during my time at Xerox. He played a huge role in my climb up the corporate ladder.

He was working as a region personnel manager in 1978. We've worked together during my time at Xerox. We were as effective in our roles as Eddie Jordan and Mike Dabney had been at Rutgers. He was the head of human resources when I was a vice president and again when I was the president of the North American Solutions Group. I hired him as a consultant when I became the CEO at Medifast, a successful weight loss company in Maryland.

I immediately witnessed Ed's work ethic and moral compass when I started working with him. I like to believe we modeled each other's good habits and counseled each other, which helped us both reach our full potential and made the company better. As Abraham Lincoln entered the Civil War to better our country, Ed similarly made decisions to better our company. His presence was a constant reinforcement of values similar to those of Bill Foster, Dick Lloyd, Joe Boylan, and Tom Young.

Ed was the son of Italian immigrants who had settled in upstate New York, where they ran a bar and restaurant. "We lived in a quintessential Italian neighborhood in Ithaca," he recalls. "It was called Little Italy. The Catholic Church was everywhere. We all attended Immaculate Conception High School and took down the bingo tables to play basketball in the gym, and had family meals Sunday after Mass. We were like a lot of first-generation families. As my brother used to say, 'I don't know if we're rich or poor. I just know we've got everything we need.'

"Economics didn't matter either when it was time to go to college. It was not an option. I went to Bentley College near Boston, which was known for its business program. The school prided itself on its career services program. I intended to go to graduate school, but when I was a senior I also took the interviews at Xerox, IBM, General Electric, and Colgate. I declined the job offers, because I wanted to return to school to get a graduate degree. But just after graduation, I got another call from Xerox. I had just moved to New York City, and they wanted me to come in for a second interview. In an Italian house, you never say no to seconds, so I took the second interview. I was hired. I was working in New York City and going through the management training school. I learned a lot working in personnel, so I settled into human resources."

During Ed's many roles in human resources, he made sure that every individual who merited an opportunity was provided one. He was recognized for implementing dynamic affirmative action programs and introducing minorities and women into the workforce.

This program would not have been successful without the leadership of Joe C. Wilson. Joe was the first modern-day CEO at Xerox. He understood the importance of Xerox's demonstrating corporate responsibility long before it was fashionable. Joe wrote a letter to all Xerox managers that he wanted an aggressive program to recruit and hire more people of color in the company. When Ed was hired, only 4 percent of Xerox employees were minorities. Through the work of many, over 50 percent of the 140,000-person workforce are now minorities. Former Xerox CEO Ursula Burns is the first woman of color to have led a Fortune 500 company.

Ed and I first met when I was selected to enroll in a program for top producers in the field. We were all being fast-tracked for management jobs and, fortunately for me, Ed was one of my teachers.

"Back then," Ed recalls, "we had an accelerated program called Management Resource Planning for anybody we felt had high potential among the sales reps. We would look at all the sales rep, sales specialists, sales managers and talk to their managers to see what their ascendency could be. Could they make the jump to two of three levels above where they were?

"Mike was a specialist at the time," he says of me, "and we had a program where we would bring in a group of men and women to the region office every month for a day and talk about every aspect of the business. Some days we would talk about management; some days we would talk about product development or pricing or marketing. We would talk about various subjects we wanted them to become astute about as they proceeded to high-level management positions. The program lasted from six to nine months. The objective was to get them ready to be sales managers, branch managers. Ten percent of those individuals would be part of the accelerated program. They were the people we chose to go to Columbia and Harvard for business and marketing courses. Mike went to both. The objective was to select the people we thought could advance to the vice presidential or presidential level.

"I quickly recognized why Mike had been invited to the program, and appreciated that he wasn't caught up in his own achievements."

When I was managing a group of frontline sales representatives, Ed suggested I get an upper-level executive to come down and meet my team. "I told Mike it would help his kids to meet the CEO and it would help him, too," he remembers. "He invited our CEO, David Kearns. David watched him lead the team meeting. And as Renée Zellweger said in *Jerry Maguire*, he had him at hello. He quickly built a relationship with David. David, too, saw Mike as an asset to Xerox. I told Mike, 'Those guys never see the lower-level people.' CEOs like to travel. They like to brag and say, 'Hey, I went to the Princeton branch and traveled with a sales rep.' David Kearns was a great CEO. There were a couple times Mike had opportunities for jobs, and he would always consult with him. In 1988, he set up a branch meeting in Princeton."

David Kearns was an inspirational leader who cared deeply about educational reform. He was a passionate champion of diversity in the workplace, and advanced Xerox to become the undisputed leader in equal opportunity employment in the 1970s and 1980s. I was a better person because of learning from him.

It appeared I had a metaphorical E-ZPass and didn't have to wait in the toll lane. But I was unaware of a supervisor of mine who didn't want to be leapfrogged. I was at a meeting celebrating the accomplishments of Xerox in 1987. But it became clear after I set up the meeting with David that my supervisor wasn't going to give me a pat on the back. And my wife was at the meeting. Then I felt like Publishers Clearing House knocked on my door. Dave got up and said, "You know, I want to thank Mike Mac-Donald for the ten years of his performance in New Jersey." Then he said, "By the way, I'm looking forward to him and Jean going up to Rochester, where I grew up." He realized that the supervisor had snubbed me the whole meeting. He sat down with my wife for almost an hour after the meeting and talked to her about living in Rochester.

Jean had never lived outside of her hometown of South River, New Jersey.

"I never thought Mike would move," Ed admits. "He was a Jersey/Philly guy, and he liked being close to his family and his in-laws."

I accepted a job as a product manager. It's been said that opportunities come at the most inopportune time. That was the case with us. We had three young children, and we didn't have a built-in support group in Rochester like we did in New Jersey. When Jean gave birth to our youngest, Chris, in New Jersey, she also needed gall bladder surgery. She spent almost a year recovering. So, I got an apartment in Rochester, New York, and commuted for a year. Jean eventually joined me with our three young kids: Ryan, Stacey, and Chris.

Rochester was a boom town located near the shores of Lake Ontario between Syracuse and Buffalo, and the greater metro area had a population of around one million people throughout six counties. It rose to prominence as the birthplace and home to three iconic companies: Xerox, Eastman Kodak, and Bausch & Lomb. Each one of those companies was a major sponsor of the U.S. Olympic teams. Wegmans, Gannett newspapers, Paychex, Western Union, French's, Constellation Brands, and Ragú also had a corporate presence in the city. Rochester became a global center for science, technology, research, and development and had a vibrant music scene.

We eventually found a nice Colonial home we liked in Pittsford, a pretty suburb with eleven parks and plenty of green space. Most important to me, it was the home of the Oak Hill Country Club, which hosted many major golf tournaments, including the PGA. The only trouble was, it became very cold with a lot of snow for long periods of time from October through May. We never got a chance to have a housewarming. The day we moved in, I was taking Ryan to Cub Scouts, and I slipped on some black ice and broke my ankle and tore the ligaments above it. I was immobilized in a full-length cast for the next six weeks. Remembering what had happened to other members on my college team, I missed only one day of work and traveled in that cast.

With the promotion, I was invited to the Advanced Management program at Columbia University. The program lasted for a month and focused on leadership in a for-profit organization and the development and implementation of that vision. Ed pushed me to go.

Business is no different than basketball or life. We all have goals. Mine was to be a top-level manager. When I worked for Jim Valvano at Iona, he used to carry a card in his pocket with a list of goals on it. "Win a national championship" was at the top of the list. To do that, Jim knew he had to sign the best recruits, including Jeff Ruland, one of the top five prospects in the country. Who the hell thought Jeff Ruland would become an Iona Gael? Not me. But Jim had a plan. And we worked that plan.

I also had a plan.

I was now swimming in unfamiliar waters. But as long as I was willing to put in the work, I was never afraid to take chances. I was swimming farther from shore, but I saw a brighter horizon.

Xerox, like basketball, was all about performance. If you worked hard and were productive, you made yourself an asset to the team and, most important, the company wouldn't want to lose you to the competition.

In 1991, I received my first vice president's job after being tapped by Emerson Fullwood, the general manager of Xerox's supply business. "I first heard about Mike when I was running one of the Xerox offices in Manhattan, and he was in New Jersey and was one of the top salespeople coming up," he recalls of me at the time. "A good friend, Tom Dolan, told me about Mike. He couldn't stop talking about him and asked me to keep an eye on him. Mike was one of those guys you always wanted on your team. He was a real company man. He'd be the first one in and the last one out of the foxhole.

"We needed a real field leader to run this operation, which consisted of one thousand people and brought in seven hundred to eight hundred million dollars in revenue to the company, and was on its way to become a one-billion-dollar division. Xerox was a performance-oriented company. Performance counted no matter how young you were, how old you were, what you looked like. Mike was on the list, but there were a couple of candidates ahead of him. I advocated for Mike with the president of U.S. operations. So, you can imagine the pressure that was on me. They wanted to wait, but I said Mike would be perfect for this vice presidential job.

"His brand was pretty strong in the company and I had enough credibility, so they appointed him. He came in and killed it.

"Mike was all about people, listening and taking action, making sure they were well-trained, well-developed, that they had a voice and made the contributions the company was looking for. The customers were king. Mike, having gone through the sales organization, knew what it meant to listen to customers in terms of the kind of products and services they wanted at the right price."

Emerson was one of the first black employees to climb the corporate ladder at Xerox. He grew up near Wilmington, North Carolina, and was one of the first to break the color barrier at North Carolina State. "I was a National Merit Scholar," he says. "There were ten of us out of fifty thousand undergraduates in those days. I graduated in 1970, went to Columbia in New York City, and joined Xerox. My wife says I married Xerox first, then I married her. I had great support from my parents. Our graduating class in high school was the last segregated class in the state, and there was a lot riding on my shoulders academically for others to come behind me. So, I wanted to be the best I could be. Fortunately, I was an acclaimed academic student there.

"When I was in graduate school, my mindset had not changed. I was driven to be the best. One of the courses I had was about the titans of business. I read about Joe Wilson of Xerox. He was such a charismatic leader. It was a young company that was growing like wildfire, very cutting-edge. I liked the values of the company. It wasn't like you had to be there ten, twenty years before you could move up in the company. I thought, 'Wow, this is the company I want to be with.' Xerox gave you the opportunity to be all you could be. I had many, many offers, but it didn't take long for me to forge my brand—who I was and what I was capable of contributing to the company—and I was recognized at a very early age. You got to do the work yourself, but it doesn't hurt to have the mentors, the sponsors.

"The analogies of sports are very similar to those of diversity where you are in a dogfight, and you got a certain group of fans pulling for you and you got a second group of fans hoping you trip up. So, you got to be really determined to be all you can be. There are so many stumbling blocks, but if you put the work in, you have a reasonably good chance to be all you can be. Life isn't fair, but at Xerox it got fairer and fairer every day. They had enlightened leadership at the top, which trickled throughout the corporation. Employees felt comfortable saying, 'Look, we have a voice and here's how we think this could be better. We want a seat at the table.' Sports have opened a lot of doors for a lot of us."

Many have stood on Emerson's shoulders since he arrived at Xerox. At the same time, Xerox promoted Kathy Lane from sales rep to its first black female sales manager. The hire was controversial, according to Ed Ciaschi.

"At the time, we only had two black female sales reps, and they were selling telecopiers," he says. "And at the time, there was a New York teacher layoff, and there were hundreds of women who had gotten out of college to teach school in Manhattan or the boroughs and they found themselves without jobs. We started searching out these women through advertising and getting them to come in for interviews. We clearly spelled out the correlation between teaching and selling.

"There was a period when Xerox and IBM were really leading the charge in bringing in African Americans, Hispanics, black women, and white women. We were breaking barriers in selling to groups they had never sold to before. They never had a black woman sell on Seventh Avenue, and we changed that. Emerson was critical in leading, helping, and bringing people aboard. He welcomed them and said, 'Hey, I know it's tough, but we can do it.'"

It was a history lesson I took with me as I moved up the chain of command and began selecting my own management teams. There were some challenges along the way.

I was working for Chuck Otto as vice president of the Eastern Region in 1991. I was thirty-eight years old and managing sales and service from Maine to Washington, D.C. It was an $850 million business.

At the time, we had nine vice presidents at my level in nine regions. I took over a region that had had negative revenue growth the year before, and the country was going through a difficult economic time. When I met with Chuck, he told me my sales budget—meaning the amount we had to sell—was up 37 percent.

"Chuck," I said, "we didn't grow at all last year."

He said to me, "Mike I think you are an up-and-coming, talented guy. I think you can do it. So, I'm giving you the highest budget in the country."

I went back and did the analysis, and discovered that all the senior guys had an average budget of 18 percent. So, I wrote him a letter. But it did not change his mind. He said, "Mike, you got to go do it."

I got together with Ed and the eight vice presidents working for me, and we plotted it out. That year, we grew the business in our region by 18 percent. We led the country in growth, but I finished seventh out of nine regional managers because our budget was so far off. When Chuck and I spoke at the end of the year, he said, "Mike, you did a terrific job. You delivered actual results. I thought you could deliver those results."

The next year, he made my budget consistent with everyone else's, and our team finished number one in the country.

The point of that story is to show that Xerox had a system in those days, in which the young guys were asked to produce even though they might not get the financial reward. I will always have great respect for Chuck Otto because he pushed me to be successful.

It was not all work and no play. Xerox is a customer-centric business.

The company was a worldwide sponsor of the Olympics for forty years. It was involved in the publication and distribution of Olympic results, and provided photocopiers and other office equipment, supplies and services to organizing committees. We also sponsored big golf and tennis events, like the U.S. Open and the PGA championship. At the time, David Myerscough was the president of North America, and I was his vice president for marketing. I was handling a lot of their sports and one of my responsibilities was running the Winter and Summer Olympic Games, taking high-profile customers to big events. We also held special events.

My favorite was the Lillehammer Winter Games in 1994. Norway is a beautiful country in Scandinavia that is famous for the Northern Lights. It can get a little cold up there. Sometimes the temperatures drop down to twenty degrees below zero Fahrenheit. For one event we were hosting, we asked one of the farmers if we could convert one of his barns into a restaurant. We took the guests out there on a bus, then put them on horse-drawn sleighs with torches to take them across the snow to dinner. We even had two of the farmer's daughters, dressed in traditional clothing, serenade the guests with Norwegian songs. We worked with NBC to get them on TV the next day.

American speed skaters were successful at Lillehammer. Bonnie Blair won two gold medals, bringing her total to five. And Dan Jansen won gold. The biggest story of the games centered around American figure skaters Nancy Kerrigan and Tonya Harding. A month before the games, Harding was implicated in an alleged plot to injure Kerrigan, her chief competitor. Harding filed a lawsuit against the U.S. Olympic Committee, seeking an injunction against being barred from the games. However, the legal dispute was temporarily put on hold. Both skaters showed up in Norway. The showdown on the ice never materialized, as Harding stumbled in her short program, finishing eighth. I was there for the finals. Although Kerrigan skated a nearly flawless long program, Oksana Baiul, a sixteen-year-old skater from Ukraine, edged her out for the gold.

Four years later, we sponsored the Boston Celtics. Carlos Pascual was the president of the North American region, and I was his chief of staff. Carlos was born in Spain and had come from Europe, where he had run two of the big worldwide organizations. He was a big soccer guy, but he didn't know anything about basketball. I flew with Carlos to Boston to cut a deal with Red Auerbach, who coached the Celtics to nine NBA championships and was the president of the team. Carlos had no idea who Red was, so I told him, "Carlos, you are going to meet the most famous pro basketball coach ever."

So, we were there negotiating the deal, and Red said to Carlos, "You guys are from Rochester. I used to come to your town to scout the Kodak Classic."

Carlos said, "Red, we're not Kodak. We're Xerox."

Everybody laughed. We agreed to sponsor the Celtics for the next four years. On the way back, we were taking the elevator and Red lit up one of his famous victory cigars.

Xerox reinforced the importance of being a lifelong learner. During the time when I was serving as the chief of staff, Ed pushed me to attend the Harvard Business School Executive Leadership program. Though I didn't keep a goals card in my sports jacket like Jim Valvano did, I had many goals and realized this program would help me achieve them.

Who would have known, after not being able to afford Princeton, I would attend two Ivy League schools?

The program lasted three months, and I had classes with people from all over the world—Australia, China, Germany, Israel. One classmate was a general from the Israeli secret service. I was talking to him and he said, "I see you have your wife, Jean, and three children." I asked him how he knew that, and he told me they did a background check on everyone. The Israelis even had security at their hotels.

Most of the people in the program were targeted to become presidents or CEOs of their companies. They came from diverse backgrounds. I was coming from sales and marketing, and there were guys there who were experts in finance, private equity, and banking. We got to listen to world-class professors from the Harvard faculty, like Michael Porter, who has written twenty books on corporate strategy. David Yoffie, the famous strategist who spent twenty-nine years on the board of Intel, would lecture on strategy, marketing, mergers and acquisitions, and implementing systems. We also spent time breaking down case studies and sharing information. For me, it was a great educational experience.

Among other things, I had a computer class for which I had to turn in assignments every night. If you didn't do well in the course, they'd tell your bosses. How'd you like to be a CEO getting a letter from Harvard saying you weren't up to snuff? Those things were risk-versus-reward. If you did well, it could help your career. If you did poorly, you could really hurt your career. That's the kind of challenge you face to be successful. It's like taking enough shots in practice to be ready to make the big one in the game.

Antonio "L.A." Reid was one of my classmates. He was a top guy in the record business. Reid and Kenneth "Babyface" Edmonds founded LaFace Records in 1989 through a joint venture with Arista Records creator Clive Davis of Atlanta. LaFace soon became one of the premier labels for popular R&B and hip-hop artists. Reid is credited with signing a fourteen-year-old Usher, whose eight albums sold eighty million worldwide.

Other popular acts on the label included Toni Braxton and TLC. Reid has won three Grammy Awards as a songwriter. Over the course of his career, he has written and produced for artists like Mariah Carey, Avril Lavigne, Pink, Justin Bieber, Rihanna, Ciara, Bobby Brown, Jennifer Lopez, Whitney Houston, and the Jacksons.

I had no knowledge of the record business, though every night Reid would talk about Michael Jackson and Pink and other celebrities. The funny thing is, he may have known less about basketball than I did about music. I really questioned my ability to teach when he never developed an interest in basketball. We were trying to watch the NBA playoffs with Michael Jordan on TV in the dorms, and he was more interested in who was singing the national anthem.

This was a great experience for me. It wasn't like Jean wasn't working. She was holding the family together, allowing me to do the things I needed to succeed in my career. I can only imagine what my parents felt when they realized their son was enrolled at Harvard.

In 1998, I felt lucky to be working at a company that was doing well. I was the number-two guy in U.S. operations.

Then Xerox hired Richard Thoman from IBM to be its new CEO in 1999. This was not a popular or productive decision. Xerox reorganized its direct sales force from a geographic structure to one based on specific industries. The decision broke the relationships between numerous customers and sales reps; it alienated customers, since many sales reps either left the company or had their territories changed. It also resulted in sales reps spending less time selling because of realignment training and increased travel time.

I was on a task force at the time, and I objected to this. I felt the company was going to go through a difficult time. I could have been fired for my views. I tried to relieve the stress by playing two-on-two basketball in our driveway with Ryan, Stacey, and their friend Jeff Brown when they were in high school. I'd work from seven in the morning until six thirty at night, then come home and lace up my sneakers, and we'd play for two hours with the lights on.

In the end, I got lucky. Xerox had a number of good people. Anne Mulcahy had been named president of general market operations, a four- to five-billion-dollar division involving all medium-size customers throughout the world. She threw me a lifeline and offered me my first president's job—in North American general marketing, a three-billion-dollar division.

It was perfect. It allowed me to focus and apply everything I had learned from my coaches and Xerox. This was when I learned the value of doing your job and focusing on the things you can control.

CHAPTER 9

Handling a Crisis

Richard Thoman was fired after thirteen months, and Anne Mulcahy was named CEO of Xerox in 2001. Although Anne saw herself humbly as the accidental CEO of Xerox, those who worked with her would strongly disagree. She reminded me a lot of Joe Torre, who had taken over as manager of the underachieving New York Yankees team in 1996 and restored them to their former glory, winning four World Series championships in eleven years. Anne had a similar type of success with our company.

In 2001, Anne was one of only three female CEOs at Fortune 500 companies. Xerox was on the verge of bankruptcy. It was not the same blue-chip company that had been valued at twenty billion dollars and had been making its shareholders an annualized return of 34 percent a year in the 1960s.

She had a Jim Valvano–like vision, work ethic, and ability to communicate with people. As part of her reorganization, she persuaded me to join her in her effort to make Xerox what it has become today. I worked for her from 1998 to 2008. During that time, as I mentioned, I became president of North American general marketing, which was responsible for the agents, the internet, and the telemarketing business at Xerox. Then I became president of the North American Solutions Group, a division that produced $6.5 billion in profits in a given year. Finally, I was the president of global accounts and marketing at a time when the company was rebranding itself.

Part of Anne's genius was creating a leadership team whose meetings may have been as spirited as her family's dinner table conversations in Rockville Centre, Long Island, or the halftime analysis by Tom Young and Joe Boylan. We all had input. She made the decisions that would take a teetering giant and nurse it back to health.

Anne understood Xerox better than anyone else. While most CEOs have stellar credentials, none could match Ann's innate knowledge of what made Xerox great.

Anne grew up with three brothers in a typical New York Irish Catholic family. She matriculated at Marymount College in Tarrytown, New York, and studied English and journalism. She went to work for Chase Manhattan bank after she graduated. "Chase Manhattan put me in human resources. I wanted to be on the banking side, but as a woman without a finance background it would have been difficult," she recalls. "I always wanted to move to their training program, where I would be given the opportunity to rotate throughout different departments in the bank. I became irritated when I realized it wasn't going to happen. It was 1974; it was more than fifty years since women had won the right to vote in 1920. I left and I needed a job.

"My brother Tom worked for Xerox, and he arranged an interview, believing my writing background would be an asset to the team. Little did Tom or I know I was interviewing for a sales job. I had no interest or motivation to be a sales rep, though I was motivated not to move back home. I didn't love sales. I became a good sales rep because I worked hard. I learned from many other people in the company. I had different skills than my brother Tom and Mike," she says, referencing me, "but I became a good sales manager because of Xerox's investment in me. When I was rewarded with a sales team after seven years, I felt I had found my calling.

"I loved leading teams. I enjoyed challenging people and celebrating when we surpassed our goals. I spent sixteen years in the field in sales before I became vice president for human resources in 1992, in charge of benefits, compensation, labor relations, and management development. In 1997, I was appointed as chief of staff to CEO Paul Allaire and was charged with leading the company's push into small-office and home-office businesses. I also took charge of Xerox's nine-hundred-fifty-million-dollar acquisition of Tektronix Inc.'s color printing and imaging division."

Like many tech companies, Xerox enjoyed a monopoly. It was a high-end copying equipment company and was raking in money for the shareholders in the sixties. But the threats to our market share became larger because of increased competition from Canon, Hewlett-Packard, Ricoh, and others, combined with the botched reorganization strategy that had cost the previous CEO his job. Sustaining business was hard enough. A weak global economy didn't help, nor did a Securities and Exchange Commission investigation into defrauding investors because of stated inflated revenue.

It was hard to imagine, but Xerox was unraveling at alarming speed in 1999 and 2000. The company was nineteen million dollars in debt, had lost money for seven straight quarters, and had only $150 million scattered around the globe. Customers had lost confidence. Employers were sprinting for greener pastures, and shareholders had seen the stock fall from sixty-four dollars to just under five dollars a share by 2001. The board knew it was time for a change, which is why it appointed Anne president and CEO in August 2001, to replace Richard Thoman.

Nobody was more surprised than Anne herself. She was only forty-eight. "The day I was named president and CEO, I'd like to say it was a lifelong dream, but that wasn't the case," Anne says. "It was a responsibility I accepted with equal parts pride and dread."

She was walking in big shoes. Xerox had a history of great CEOs, especially David Kearns, who was now was dying. He was eighty years old and had sinus cancer. He could barely see, having lost his left eye during radiation surgery in 1993; he wore an eyepatch the rest of his life. David had been good to me when I was coming up through the ranks. After he retired, he would still go to Stamford, Connecticut, to work out in the gym. Tom Dolan and I walked in one night, and there was David. "Hello, Mr. Kearns. Hello, Mr. Kearns," we said.

He immediately recognized our voices. "Mike, Tom, how you guys doing?" he said. It was one of those moments you never forget.

Anne wasn't fazed by a changing of the guard.

Though the Sacred Heart sisters hadn't offered any alchemy classes at Marymount, Anne had the qualities that Xerox badly needed at that time. She was smart, brutally honest, hardworking, disciplined. She valued the employees as much as the technology. According to a story in *Fortune* magazine, she had the integrity of a sixteen-year-old Catholic school girl. She was described as compassionate but tough. She was willing to leave her office in Stamford, roll up her sleeves, and work with her employees in the field. That gave her instant street credibility. And the employees wanted to follow her if it meant Xerox would survive.

She won the hearts of her people because she cared so much. Maybe it was that old Catholic guilt, but she would lie in bed at night thinking about the ninety-six thousand employees and what would happen if Xerox went south. Entire families worked for Xerox—including her brother Tom and husband, Joe, who retired in 1998 after a thirty-five-year sales career. When Anne was offered the job, she took it out of loyalty to her coworkers even though she had not been prepped for it.

"They were hungry for leadership," she says. "I was able to fill a void and benefited from my background in human resources. It could be said I was ahead of the curve, but I wasn't going to ask someone to do what I wouldn't do. And they responded. Now it's more common to get out into the field. At the time, most CEOs were not doing that. I am not sure my style would have worked in other places, but I think Xerox was uniquely positioned. I never thought about whether there had been discrimination against women in the past. There was no time for it. It was tougher externally than internally, but having people like Mike on my team helped," she recalls of me. "They were ahead of their time. They were enlightened. They were in a company that had values for so long that a lot of traditional male executives would have had trouble with that. They didn't blink.

"It was special and an early model for what we should all be aspiring to."

One of the many reasons Anne was successful is that she knew what she didn't know. With limited experience in financial accounting, she knew it was important to use the talents of Joe Mancini, the director of corporate financial analysis, who showed her how to navigate the company's thirty-billion-dollar balance sheet and tutored her in the finer points of finance before meetings with the company's bankers. She took home binders and crammed before meetings with the forty-seven Xerox bankers.

Some on the board were recommending that the best way to resurrect the company was to file for bankruptcy. I think Anne would have rather conceded an arm-wrestling competition to her brothers. She would never be outworked or doubt the people she had hired in human resources. One of the first things she did was meet with the top one hundred executives in the company and tell them straight up how bad things had become. Ninety-eight percent of them decided to stay and work with her.

I was one of them.

I first met Anne at a Xerox ski event in Vermont in the eighties and was friends with her brother. I felt I connected with her because of our similar backgrounds. I admired her confidence and felt I would help the company when she offered me the job of president of the North American Solutions Group. "Mike was an easy hire," she says of choosing me for the job. "I knew he was loyal and had the respect of others, and he wouldn't be afraid to make the tough decisions we needed to be successful."

I was lucky. I had worked for a woman in New Jersey, Kathy Mullaly, who was one of the youngest woman managers at Xerox when I was a sales manager. She was from Long Island and had worked in New York City for years. So, when I worked with Anne, it wasn't a new experience. I had a good experience with Kathy and a better one with Anne. I never had any issues with her. She had great intrapersonal skills, good vision, and leadership skills, and she gave us room to operate. She had that ability to give directions and she was there for us, but she didn't get in the way. She empowered me, and I empowered my people. It was a lot like my last Rutgers team. Everyone had a role and knew what it was. In any organization, executing your role is important. She recognized people for their performance. She was trustworthy; she had high ethics and integrity. The two most important things in a company like Xerox are culture and truth.

Anne personified an incredible work ethic. In her first year, she and I each logged over a hundred thousand miles in air travel, and we separately visited every Xerox office location in the country. She believed in getting feedback from people at all levels at Xerox as well as meeting customers. It was because of this that we had confidence in her decisions that others might have considered risky. She also gained the confidence of banks, who were willing to give her an infusion of cash. She took out a one-billion-dollar loan—and then another. She recognized the importance of research and development, which was the long-term future of the company.

This time of restructuring forced Anne to eliminate some positions.

When I became president of the North American Solutions Group, the company was going through this downsizing. We had to cut five hundred million dollars from our budget in a two-year period. I had the unwelcome job of laying off one thousand of our two thousand employees at Xerox headquarters. We also had to address the fact that because we were getting into digital copiers, we needed to reduce the number of technicians in the field because we didn't have the workload for them anymore.

Vice president of human resources Ed Ciaschi, CFO Pat Fulford, and I decided to arrange a meeting to talk about reductions. We thought it would be better not to have it in Rochester, for confidentiality reasons. We decided to take the senior leadership team from headquarters down to Myrtle Beach, South Carolina, to make some tough decisions and come up with a plan.

Not to minimize it, but this experience gave me a small amount of insight into what the freshman coaches at Bonner went through when they had to make massive cuts during tryouts. We all loved basketball back then, just like these guys loved the company now. I called everyone in the building to a meeting at an auditorium at Xerox Tower. I wanted to be straight with them. "Look, this company is in trouble," I said. "These are things we've got to do." I looked out at everyone in the room and said, "Only fifty percent of you are going to be here after three months."

Then I said, "I'm going to help you with severance and job placement service. I want to let you all know I've got to take these actions for the good of the company."

I eventually reduced employees in the division from 51,000 to 27,000.

This was a notch no one wanted in their belt, though years later, people told me I was one of the few executives who worked with his employees to make help them make a transition in their careers. It was something that Anne did too. And it wasn't taught in my Harvard classes. Having played on a number of teams, I realized we were all in this together.

But at the time, it was extremely difficult.

I lived in Pittsford, as I mentioned, which was basically a Xerox and Kodak subdivision. My kids went to school with many children whose parents were given pink slips. I got threats. I had to have an armed guard on my floor. In the office, I was encouraged to take precautions because no one knew what could happen. We felt we had done all a company could do for its employees, but we still didn't know if we were in danger.

It's easy to talk about numbers, but when your teammates have faces, it's painful. But the company was fighting for survival. If we did not make the cuts and the corporation failed, then everyone would be out of a job. I decided to generate cash and profitability and have the corporation succeed and think about rebuilding. I had confidence in Anne and our management team. We were going to get it done.

I still feel sad about that. Letting all those people go was the most difficult thing I've ever had to do in my life.

Fortunately, we were able to manage.

There were also changes in the senior management team. This was not unlike my own experience as a recruited athlete. My role changed in each of my four years at Rutgers, just as it was necessary for vice presidents to adapt to the new environment. The same principles apply. Just as on a team, some members helped us. Others couldn't and had to be cut. There was a different culture when the company was thriving than when it was in financial trouble. Some executives couldn't handle the bumps in the restructuring road. There is a certain type of person who can come back from a halftime deficit, figure out what needs to be done, create the right strategy, and then execute it.

I worked with Ed and we put together a strong, diverse senior staff. We assembled a better recruiting class than even Dick Vitale had. We brought in "prime-time players" like Valerie Blauvelt from marketing; Rick Cerrone, who ran the supply business; Mike Branningan from sales; and Mike Ianacone, a vice president who had gone from the Eastern Region to run market operations in headquarters.

Though we were all cut from the same cloth, we all had different backgrounds. Some people were white. Some were black. Some were men. Some were women. Some were in the field. Fortunately, we were all invested in the process.

"Mike surrounded himself with great people," Ed recalls of my choices. "He always valued other people's opinions and considered them when he made decisions."

We didn't want to hire minorities and just put them in the corner. Frank Edmonds and Larry Thompson ran the East and the West, which generated three-quarters of our revenue. And one of the people who made our team great was Lynn Carter, who was senior vice president in charge of graphic communications, which was responsible for three to four billion dollars in business. I realized no one knew the industry better.

Lynn grew up in Coatesville, Pennsylvania, a steel town thirty-nine miles west of Philadelphia. She started her professional career as a stenographer for Lukens Steel working in the main office, which was considered a big deal for a young black woman. I admired her drive. She quickly decided she wanted more. She went to school at night at Immaculata University and West Chester University and worked her way up to being a customer service representative and having clients all over the country. But she reached a "steel ceiling" at Lukens and was hired by Xerox in 1977, and worked her way up to the executive level. She was headquartered in Washington, D.C., and finished her undergraduate degree at American University.

"Mike always was an inspiration in terms of communicating what had to be done," she says of my management style. "He always drafted the best players. When he was talking to his team, he always laid out what the goals were and then told you why. You were judged on the skills and competency you brought to the organization. I worked for Mike three or four times. He always struck a special chord with you. He always respected you. You didn't have to change who you were. You could bring your best self. There weren't any prima donnas. Mike wasn't going to put up with that. We were all on one team, and the competition was on the outside.

"America today has lost that sense. In the social media world, people are more consumed with themselves than how they can work to help a company. A rising tide raises all boats. We were all successful when we worked for Mike. There was never a doubt Mike was not going to credit our success to anyone who didn't earn it."

We relied a lot on the Leadership Diamond developed by the great business philosopher Peter Koestenbaum to kick-start the recovery. The Leadership Diamond is a model of the leadership mind and a method for expanding leadership. It distinguishes four independent leadership imperatives—ethics, vision, courage, and reality—that all lead to greatness.

We knew what the vision was, and we had to change things. We needed to have the courage to do it, but we also needed to take a realistic look at the situation and say, "If we don't do this, we're done."

Leaders lead. You need to take a visionary approach, and you can't let it become personal. You make a business decision. One of the things I've always tried to do is separate business from my personal feelings.

It gave us a framework to work from. When you are a leader, you need to look at yourself and say, "Do I have the vision of what I'm doing? How are my ethics? Do I have the courage to make decisions?" Then there's the reality: "Can I do it? Can I get it done?"

I prioritized and dealt with everyone equally, whether it was a big account like Kinko's or small entrepreneurs. A turnaround doesn't happen in the office, so we had to be sure we were out in the field. We had a lot of partners. We were doing color, art. It was different, and it was exciting.

We were all focused on the same goal.

Although just like at the College Avenue gym at Rutgers, it didn't look that way when we first started. I wasn't able to complete my first meeting. Joe Valenti, a good friend who was the senior vice president of our service group and was responsible for twenty thousand technicians and print shop employees, was on a fishing trip in Canada and broke his leg. He came back and went to the hospital. The doctors were getting ready to operate on his leg. They gave him anesthesia and he died. He had an enlarged heart. They hadn't realized it. I found this out during the meeting and excused myself, went to the hospital, and spent time with Joe's widow and the family. We eventually hired Bill Steenburgh from Kodak as his replacement. He had two brothers who were executives at Xerox.

Just as I felt like we were gaining traction, I, like the rest of the world, was forced to deal with the attacks on the World Trade Center in 2001. The day it happened, I was playing an early round of golf with Pat Martin, the CEO of StorageTek, in Rochester. We played nine holes. I went into the clubhouse and saw the planes crashing into the towers on TV. I immediately called Ed, and we created a crisis center. I was worried about the seventy-five employees who were scheduled to work in the Twin Towers. I wanted to contact every one of them to find out where everybody was. We got in touch with seventy-three. Unfortunately, the two we didn't contact died. One didn't have a phone. He was working in one of the print centers and perished. The other was a twenty-six-year-old guy from Newark who had just started with us. He was killed trying to help people out of the buildings.

Xerox was lucky. If that had happened a half hour later, it would have been much worse. My New York managers were in a meeting in Chicago, and got in a car and drove back. Later that week, I flew to Westchester and met with the team that handled accounts in the Financial District and knew people who had died. I went down to our service center near the Twin Towers. The streets smelled of death. I wanted to do more.

Those were stressful times. We were all working twenty-four/seven. "I would talk to Mike at least three times a week during that period," Anne recalls of our communications. "I'd call at seven thirty in the morning and seven thirty at night, and he'd be in the office picking up the phone."

To prepare people to be successful, I learned, they had to be trained and recognized for their achievements. It was important that our team members felt like they were part of something bigger than themselves. I ran cruises around the world for top-producing vice presidents. I sent our top managers to the Center for Creative Leadership in Greensboro, North Carolina, which provided them with the ability to be their best, and provided me with the insight to know who had the potential to be leaders in the organization.

The corporation had four major objectives—customer satisfaction, employee satisfaction, business results, and process management—that Anne wanted implemented.

"Those objectives were reinforced by Mike's management style," Mike Ianacone recalls of my process. "Mike understood headquarters and the field very well. He had built a strong team around him, and he knew when and where to take actions when he needed to make tough decisions. He managed performance, held people accountable, and recognized achievement. Throughout the process, he had the courage to do the right thing. He knew how to establish cooperation."

My success was due to my presence in the field and not allowing the stress that the members of the leadership team were feeling affect our efforts. Every organization looks to its leaders to set the tone by their own performance. We all stayed calm through tough situations. You need to be cool about how you approach things, or it will cause unrest. Good leaders aren't about giving orders. They are about getting employees to want to follow them.

I tried to apply the same philosophy to my family. It was important to maintain a balance between my professional and personal life. My oldest son, Ryan, once commented, "No matter what kind of stress my dad had during that time at Xerox, at home we never realized the challenges he faced in a day."

Ed and I would leave Monday and travel three to four days a week. We would visit all our offices. Half the day, we would meet with our employees.

It was important to understand the challenges they faced. The other half of the day, we'd meet with customers to understand the marketplace. At night, we'd take the whole management team to dinner. Then I'd go to the next city. It was a good way to get a handle on what was going on.

One of the biggest challenges was to separate fact from fiction and implement the next steps we needed to be successful.

I was always results-oriented. I would meet with a lot of managers who would give these great slide presentations. Then I'd ask them about their performance, and they'd say, "Not very good." I'd tell them, "Put away your slides; it's time to try something new. You need to do something different, or you're not going to be effective. You need to get results."

What some people don't understand in business is if you're out there and the company is failing, then the executives have failed. You've got a good brand, you've got technology, you've got a good opportunity. You've got to make it work.

A lot of management is about creating a way to make things happen, not unlike the way my mother found ways to buy Christmas presents for the family. If you don't push, you don't borrow, it's not going to happen. Ed and I were always honest with our employees. That didn't mean we weren't tough with them in reviews. Conversations could become difficult if we needed the team to do better. No matter how difficult the conversation, I always sent a letter the next day outlining a way for the individual to help himself or herself and the company. Ed would reiterate all the positives as well as the skills that needed some work.

The turnaround was driven by a very disciplined, well-thought-out approach. It was the realization of how bad things were and trying not to sugarcoat the situation. We knew we had to reduce costs, change our products—and do it in a hurry. If you don't have constant communication in a turnaround, it's not going to work. People are going to leave. We were able to keep the bulk of our key people and start to deliver results. We went from negative revenue to positive revenue, from declining profits to growing profits. We were able to change the whole business trajectory.

Things began to turn around in 2002 to 2003. With the SEC matter in the rearview mirror, Anne was able to recruit a new CFO, Larry

Zimmerman, a former vice president of finance from IBM. The company had considered many ways to improve its balance sheet, but Anne and Larry decided not to move the debt off the sheet. During this period, Xerox signed a deal with the lending arm of GE for a five-billion-dollar revolving line of credit. Margins improved, and Anne was successful in managing costs by restructuring the company. Our investment in personnel also enabled us to win back the loyalty of our customers. There was a great deal of pride at Xerox. Customers recognized the quality. We were also able to stay competitive because of Anne's decision to keep research and development a priority. She poured one billion dollars into R&D. Anne earned everyone's respect, including mine.

She made sure that she listened to everyone's concerns, so we were all moving in the same direction at the same time. She empowered the entire management team.

In my four years as president of the North America Solutions Group, our division took profits from $180 million to $680 million. We were recognized as the top-performing division in two of those years, 2001 and 2002, and achieved our goals in all four, increasing revenue from negative 8 to 5 percent.

It was a high-pressure job. I enjoyed the success, but by the end, I was worn out. The job was also taking a physical toll on my body. I had developed acid reflux disease, and it was so bad that one night when I was out to dinner, I had to be taken to the hospital. I thought I was having a heart attack. It was atrial fibrillation, a heart problem that could lead to a stroke. I went to Anne and told her I would be more effective coming off the road. She appointed me the president of worldwide marketing at corporate headquarters in Stamford. I was living in New York City. At the time, two of my children were attending college in Stamford, so I was able to spend a little more time with them. I stayed in that job four years and realized that after thirty-three years at Xerox, it was time to leave. It was nice knowing when I left Xerox in 2009 that the company was enjoying the same success as it had when Xerox first hired me in 1977.

Anne was the first woman to be selected CEO of the Year by *Chief Executive* magazine, that same year. She rebuilt Xerox, increasing the employee numbers to 150,000, which allowed it to buy other companies and grow. When she retired in 2010, she made even more history when she passed the position to Ursula Burns, the first woman of color to lead a company of that magnitude, in the first woman-to-woman succession at a Fortune 500 company. She left knowing she had led Xerox back from the brink of insolvency to profitability and restored its global image, demonstrating that a woman could succeed at the highest level of business.

Working with Anne was as good as working with Jim Valvano. Jim believed he could win a national championship. Anne believed she could move mountains.

And they both were right.

CHAPTER 10

The Legacy

Business life can be unpredictable. When I left Xerox, I still had some gas in the tank. I enjoyed doing some consulting work for Automatic Data Processing. Then, Ravi Saligram, the CEO of OfficeMax, offered me an executive vice president's position with the goal of turning around the company. It was back to the future and a restructuring of different divisions. With my experience, we believed we could improve the financials. The company was based in Chicago, and Jean and I leased an apartment on the seventy-sixth floor of the Trump Tower on the Magnificent Mile overlooking Lake Michigan. Our lease was month-to-month, because I planned to eventually return to New Jersey once we had repositioned the company.

They barely dropped the green flag in October 2011 when I got a call from my big brother, Brad.

I was in the middle of a board meeting when Brad's number appeared on my cell phone, which was unusual during the day.

Brad, who was the executive chairman of the board at Medifast, a growing weight-loss product company based in Maryland, was on the line. He gave me the worst news possible. He had terminal esophageal cancer.

I was devastated. OfficeMax was great about it and told me to take as much time as I needed. Jean and I flew to Glen Burnie, near Baltimore, the next day, then drove over to Owings Mills to meet him. When I arrived at his home, he was busy working with other members of the Medifast leadership team. Brad excused himself from the meeting and asked me to take a walk with him.

We took a three-hour walk, just the two of us. We talked about his condition, and he told me he did not think he was going to make it. He told me he was going to do everything he could, including taking experimental drugs, but he confessed it was a long shot.

"Realistically," he said, "I think I have only six months to live."

Then he asked me to take over his role at Medifast. Though I was in shock, he was still selling. He pitched me on the fact that Medifast had a $250 million market cap. He needed someone with big business experience who could take the company to the next level. God bless Brad, but the position was not what I expected.

But this was about my brother Brad asking me to do something for him.

Family means everything to me. Brad had been my role model. Now, he wanted me to carry the baton for him. Brad had a larger-than-life personality and was one of the straightest arrows I ever met, with a never-give-up attitude, which he originally got from sports.

He was competitive, especially in baseball and basketball. He had twenty close friends, and they were all the same way in any sport they played. He also got it from the Marine Corps. He enlisted after graduating from Villanova. In addition to loving America, he had a great respect for my grandfather and two uncles—who, as I mentioned, all served in World War I. Brad looked up my grandfather's military record and thought he had a tremendous career. He was influenced by our family history. Villanova has the second most successful Marine ROTC program after the Naval Academy in producing officers to advance to high levels. It was a positive experience for him. He went to ROTC camps in the summer during college. He was a big, well-built guy—six foot three, 210 pounds—who loved the friendships he made and the physical challenges he faced in the Marines.

Outwardly, there was no doubt that serving two tours at the end of the Vietnam War and again as a battalion commander in the first Gulf War helped him build upon the foundation my parents gave us. He eventually reached the rank of colonel during twenty-seven years of service to our country. I also believed he was grounded because he spent time in the Augustinian order before he married Shirley and had two daughters. The values of the Marine Corps were evident in everything Brad did—honor, courage, and commitment. He was also influenced by the values he learned at Villanova—truth, unity, and love. He always found time for others. He served on many charity boards in Baltimore and was a vice president for the Marine Corps Reserve Toys for Tots foundation.

The Marine Corps was a big part of his life. Even after he was married, he would go to reserve duty two weekends a month to run operations. He was up for general, but he was passed over a couple of times.

Then he decided to retire, because if you are a general, even in the reserves, you must work in the military for half the year. It is difficult to run any kind of business on a part-time basis.

And by that time, Brad had been bitten by the entrepreneurial bug.

He began his business career in consumer products with Carnation in New Hampshire. He started in sales, rose to sales management at Carnation, then moved to Andrew Jergens Company in Cincinnati, where he became a product manager at corporate headquarters. He was then recruited by the Bonneau Company in Texas to become the national account manager for its sunglasses business. He eventually became president of the company. He had an outgoing personality and was a great salesman—aggressive. I think Brad would have been successful selling anything. He used to source all the glasses, and he would go to China and all over the Far East. He used to run a lot of trade shows in New York City. He took Bonneau from a small company—maybe ten million dollars in sales—to one hundred million dollars before taking on the challenges at Medifast.

We had more than our business interest in common. We were friends and played golf all the time. Golf eventually replaced basketball as the sport in our family. He enjoyed coming out to the Xerox-sponsored

Phoenix Open with my younger brother, Bob; my cousin Bud; and my oldest son, Ryan. We played three rounds on the course from Sunday through Tuesday before the pro-am. Brad was about an eighteen to twenty handicap, but he loved to play because he loved sports. One time, we were on the course and Brad and Bobby looked like they were in position for a birdie, and they were laughing after Ryan, the best golfer on our family, hit a shot behind a cactus. You should have seen the expressions on their faces when Ryan hit a shot out of the sand and holed it.

Brad was a lot like my parents in that the door was always open. He owned a home in Ocean City, Maryland. We would spend many summers with Bobby and our sisters Margaret and Florence for family reunions.

What I did not realize until my walk with Brad that day was that everything he owned was invested in Medifast. He told me, "My family needs someone who will look out for them. If this goes the wrong way, our family could be in big trouble. I need somebody I trust.'"

We spent a lot of time talking about it. There was no other decision to be made. I had to take the job. It was not only a responsibility to his family but to do something for Brad the way he had always helped me.

With the efficiency of a Marine Corps drill sergeant, he went right into his office and drew up a contract after our walk.

I flew back to Chicago and resigned.

When I started at Medifast, I had no idea where I was going to live and how I was going to run the company. Brad took his family to Florida and decided to go through chemotherapy at a hospital there. Johns Hopkins sent the medicine, so he did not have to return to Baltimore and sit around in the cold weather. I decided to commute between the company headquarters and my winter home in Florida two weeks a month over the next four months. Brad was going to treatments every two days at Singer Island, where he had a condo. I'd meet him there, and he would give me a crash course on the Medifast business model during the five or six hours he was sitting in the chair.

He was the expert. I had to learn all about consumer products. I had never been involved in consumer products before. I had never been involved in retail. At Iona, we had been selling New York. At Xerox, we had been selling technology. Here we were selling a healthy lifestyle, and there was a difference in the delivery methods. At Xerox, our sales force had been our delivery method. Coaches are the delivery mechanism in weight loss.

There was a steep learning curve. Brad would spend time talking to me and giving me his insights on how the business worked. "Well, here's how our clinic works; here's how our coaching model works; here's how our doctors work," he would say. His experience in the supply chain helped him with four different sales channels. It was not easy. It was complex stuff, because we were balancing the profitability of each channel and deciding where to invest our money.

My brother was a smart guy and a high-risk taker, and someone who was also very tough in business when he had to be. He told me, "Mike, don't try to run this like your Xerox sales teams." It really made me think and focus on the different cultures and how the Medifast business operated.

Medifast was founded under the name Jason Company in 1980 by James W. Vitale. Vitale's father, a Baltimore dermatologist, had been interested in the problem of obesity. In the mid-seventies, he began treating patients using a liquid-diet plan, which imposed strict rules on doctors. But the product was difficult to obtain.

Sensing a business opportunity, Dr. Vitale began developing a new liquid-diet formula in his kitchen with a blender. The result eventually became Medifast. Dr. Vitale sold weight-loss products like diet shakes and nutrition bars through a network of doctors, who prescribed them to clinically obese patients.

At first, it was a father-and-son business. James Vitale left the home remodeling business he was in to help with his father's one-man production and marketing department. Business took off after Jason ran an ad in a medical journal; sales grew to one million dollars by the second year and then rose to seventeen million dollars.

The younger Vitale was joined by his two sisters, and the three shared ownership of Jason after they bought their father out. The weight-loss industry at the time was powered by results and celebrity endorsements.

In 1988, Oprah Winfrey, a popular TV talk host and one of the biggest influencers in the world, lost sixty pounds on a diet plan and the media chronicled her weigh-ins. The public reaction created a boom for companies in the meal-replacement industry, and Jason's sales leaped to fifty-one million dollars. Its employees grew to three hundred when the company moved to spacious offices in Owings Mills. But the market tanked when Oprah put the weight back on. In 1992 the Federal Trade Commission found Jason Pharmaceuticals, Inc. guilty of misleading advertisements about the safety and effectiveness of its products and programs. Insurers began to step away, and Jason filed for bankruptcy in 1994.

Then Brad stepped in.

At the time he learned about Medifast, he was working for the U.S. Mint, making commemorative coins for the 1996 Olympics. Two private equity guys from New York City, who were looking to build the company, recognized his leadership qualities. They approached him about being the CEO of the company, which was then known as HealthRite. Brad liked the fact that the company offered a product that was endorsed by doctors. He was intrigued by the science behind the product.

But it was by no means a blue-chip company.

Brad jumped in with both feet in 1996. Like Anne Mulcahy on a smaller scale, he had to resolve some accounting issues. When Brad came on board, he immediately confronted the company leadership. He wanted changes made. They fired him.

But just as Brad always did, he fought back. In 1997, he staged a proxy fight to take control of the company. He did an outstanding job working with the investors. He also made a big financial investment in the company himself, showing he was committed. Then he asked the investors for a similar commitment.

He garnered enough support from shareholders on his side that he won. Then he dumped all of HealthRite's failing divisions. But that didn't mean the company was going to be a success. Even though revenues went up from $14.4 million in 1997 to $15.6 million the next year, Brad's team dwindled from two hundred to one hundred. During the next five years, Brad managed to fight off bankruptcy.

Brad had shared these challenges with me at different times. He had always been a risk taker. He wanted to make this company work. He invested his sweat as well as his equity. He sold his house. He was living in a two-bedroom condo with his wife and two daughters just so he could buy more shares of the company and have more control. When he did it, I could not believe it. He raised an additional twenty million dollars to keep the company afloat. He had Shirley handling the accounting and paying the bills. One of his daughters, Meg, who had earned an undergraduate degree at Villanova and a master's degree at Loyola University Maryland, was moonlighting while working at a law firm. She followed her dad's lead and ran the supply chain. His other daughter, Kelly, who had graduated from Rosemont College, worked in business development. It was not the business campus I had known at Xerox. The company didn't have preferred vendors. But we had old friends, and Brad didn't hesitate to call on them, like the time when he had a problem with the bathroom and brought one of his buddies from Upper Darby down to fix the toilet and paid him in beer.

The magnitude of the risk he was taking was not something I would have done.

Brad, however, made this a family project.

More than Brad's pride and money were involved. He believed Medifast could change lives.

Brad knew he had to restructure the company and how it did business. He decided that the business needed to change its distribution method— selling directly to consumers, not to doctors. He invested in a call center to handle customer service and added new e-commerce functions to the company website. As a result, after falling as low as $3.9 million in 2000, sales climbed to $5 million in 2001. Then he changed the name from HealthRite to Medifast.

Dr. Wayne Scott Andersen helped Medifast take the next step.

Dr. Andersen, the first person in his family to attend college, was the chairman of the Department of Anesthesiology and director of critical care for a hospital in Dayton, Ohio, and was one of only ten board-certified doctors in critical care in the country. But he was tired of reacting to disease. "I've always been passionate about what I do and about taking care of people, but I was tired of getting up every day to put Band-Aids on people without actually addressing the root cause of their ailments," he says.

Dr. Andersen decided to get into weight loss and lifestyle change. His idea was making people healthy so they would not get sick. In his mind, optimal health was linked to the ability to achieve and maintain a healthy weight.

"My wife, Lori, who worked as a nurse in a hospital, noticed the size of my scrubs was getting bigger," Dr. Andersen recalls. "I had put on some weight from the stress of the job and didn't like the idea of not being there for my family, which included two young children. It was obvious I needed a change. I had met Brad by chance through an immunologist who was a mutual friend. He was looking for a way to expand his business and asked if I would like to talk."

Brad set up an initial meeting right after September 11, 2001. "I remember getting on a flight from Portland, Oregon, to Baltimore. I was the only one on the plane," Dr. Andersen says. "We met at the Medifast facility. There was literally nothing there—a half-empty warehouse. I remember walking in and thinking, 'What am I doing here?' They put me in a little conference room. The Formica was peeling from the tables. There were all these little boxes with 'Medifast' on them. They reminded me of a little kids' lunch boxes. I thought, 'I should run.'

"Then Brad came in. He looked like he was at a casting call for the Tom Cruise movie *A Few Good Men*. Real tall. Hair so thick. We had a great conversation. I was impressed by his passion, his knowledge, and his desire to do things the right way. We talked. I told him this plan could be a way to create a healthier world. He was not deterred by the financial state the business was in at that time. He persisted and convinced me to attend the 2002 Super Bowl with him and Mike for a second meeting. Though skeptical, I accepted the invitation to come to New Orleans.

"It was an incredible experience. The Patriots defeated the Rams, 20–17. U2 played at halftime, and there was a salute to the 3,500 people who had died in the 9/11 attacks. Afterwards, we went to dinner and

Archie Manning was a guest at our table. Also, there was one of our physicians who had won a contest for producing the most revenue in the previous year. During dinner, I pitched Brad and Mike on the idea of creating a personal coach-to-client system. Brad liked the idea because he believed obesity was a medical problem."

Dr. Andersen's initiative was launched in the basements of two residential houses in Oregon, where he lived. He also opened a call center in Utah, where he trained several members of his team on how to talk to people about health. He promised Medifast that each client would receive proper and individualized support, so his wife, Lori, interviewed every person who joined the program. Within a year, the operation had grown so big that Medifast asked Dr. Andersen to become its medical director as a subcontractor. Take Shape for Life opened in 2002 with Brad and Dr. Andersen as cofounders.

The company claimed it was about more than weight loss. The formulated meal plan focused on lifestyle changes to help people lose weight. Take Shape for Life included weekly support calls from doctors, nurses, and dietitians as well as access to an online community.

To ensure success, Brad hired Dr. Larry Cheskin from the Johns Hopkins weight management center in Baltimore as a consultant to teach Dr. Andersen about weight loss. Brad taught Dr. Cheskin about Medifast. The next big step was hiring Dan Bell. If Dr. Andersen validated the science, Dan was his equivalent in network marketing.

This was just another example of Brad's getting other people to believe in his vision for the company.

Dr. Andersen was charged with figuring out how to build a working model for the enterprise. He created a division of health care professionals in which doctors and chiropractors encouraged the habits of health.

Coaches received compensation from sales of meal replacements sold. Dr. Andersen became such an expert in the field that he wrote a book, titled *Dr. A's Habits of Health*, which made it to the *New York Times* bestseller list. He is an amazing speaker, and whenever he would get up at our conventions, he would captivate thousands of people and constantly receive standing ovations.

Take Shape for Life brought in meaningful revenue in 2003, its first year, and took off from there.

The reason for its success was the coach system, which created the ability to expand distribution. Coaches are basically people who want to be helpful. They want to pay it forward. Medifast is not a typical diet program. You've got to eat a prescribed number of Medifast meals a day depending on the program and drink a lot of water; you've got to follow a program. It takes coaching to help people reach their goals. Those coaching calls are great, because if someone doesn't know how to do it, they can ask their coach questions. The coaches will even help people make the food and recommend healthy meals.

The coaches talk to one another. If they're successful using the product, they'll talk about it to other people who want to lose weight. The program spread because of word of mouth and credibility based on success.

Somebody must have been watching.

Brad was named Young Entrepreneur of the Year in Maryland by Ernst & Young in 2006 for the customer products category after the company attained twenty-seven consecutive quarters of growth and revenues reached seventy-four million dollars.

There are an unlimited number of potential customers in the forty-billion-dollar weight loss industry. In the U.S., two-thirds of adults are either overweight or obese, and 17 percent of adolescents and children ages five and older are overweight. Individuals who are obese have a significantly increased risk of death from all causes compared to those who maintain a healthy weight.

The giants like Jenny Craig control the market, but in the early 2000s the competition was growing more intense, and Medifast's rivals—LA Weight Loss and Nutrisystem—were bulking up spending. But we felt we provided more support because of the coaching.

My brother and I were cut from the same cloth. We were always looking for an advantage. In 2007, on the advice of Father Donald Riley, who was working at Villanova at the time, Brad set up a strategic planning meeting at the business school at which he asked students there how he should grow the company. They suggested aggressively marketing

Medifast products over the internet. The strategy worked. Sales went from zero to millions of dollars in that part of the business. The stock went from nearly nothing to thirty dollars a share in December 2009.

My brother experienced some heart problems that year. He wasn't feeling good and needed a couple of stents. He wanted to spend more time in Florida with his wife. I understood it more than anyone. He took a step back, handing over the CEO job to Mike McDevitt Jr., a young private equity analyst at the Blackstone Group in New York City, whose father had gone to school with Brad. Mike McDevitt came to Medifast with a reputation for being a good financial guy, and Brad settled into the job as chairman of the board. Brad knew his strengths but also realized others' talents. He trusted Mike with being the voice of the company, though he was always in control. It was the Marine in him. He didn't want to spend much time on Wall Street. He just wanted to run the company. He knew what to do on a day-to-day basis, and he wanted to be involved in every aspect of the business.

Brad must have done something right. Medifast had grown to $105 million in revenue by 2008 as a direct result of the coaching network maturing. Looking at the success of our company, when the network grew, the stock went up. Dr. Andersen (now "Dr. A") took the network from seven thousand to ten thousand coaches. That was a big jump.

By 2010, Medifast was named the number-one small company in America by Forbes.

The success of the company was due in part to Brad's creation of varied business channels. The products were available online, through Take Shape for Life coaches, through weight-loss centers, and through doctors. Take Shape for Life had grown to ten thousand coaches. Brad felt Villanova could aid in his crusade. That same year, he founded the Mac-Donald Center for Obesity Prevention and Education at the Villanova nursing school.

The center was funded by Take Shape for Life and the MacDonald Family Foundation. It advises on the latest developments in combating the epidemic of weight gain.

Though the company was doing well, my brother was getting sicker. It was one of the worst things I experienced in my life. I can remember our last dinner, when he could barely swallow his soup.

Dr. A also spent time with Brad and me at this time. We all sat on the porch of his condo in Florida. Brad told him not to worry about anything. I would take care of the business side of the company. "For me, it was sad, but I was fortunate Mike was succeeding him," Dr. A says about that time. "I wanted our families to build a legacy together.

"Mike told me, 'I'm going to be here. We'll work together, make it fun, and do it the right way.'"

There was never a doubt Brad was in charge, up to the very end. He died in April 2012 at the age of sixty-four. He had a huge Rolodex, and he orchestrated his own funeral. The funeral Mass was held at his parish church in Baltimore. He was given full military honors. His service was attended by many generals and Cardinal Edwin F. O'Brien of Baltimore.

When we were growing up above the clothing store in Upper Darby, the paths we would take and the lessons we would learn would lead to our careers' becoming intertwined. I met many influential and successful people through basketball and Xerox. Brad ranked at the top of the list. He challenged me. He cared for me. And he was the big brother everybody wanted.

CHAPTER 11

Solving a Problem

When I assumed the leadership role at Medifast, it was bittersweet, seeing how the company had evolved so much as Brad had envisioned. This success, though welcome, came with challenges.

Medifast had quickly outgrown the capability of the management team. My goal was fueled by my promise to my brother. I was ambitious enough to believe we could take Medifast from a small company to a one-billion-dollar corporation with a worldwide reach within the next five years.

I probably sounded like Jim Valvano.

But there was a great deal to be done. We had to put a plan together to reach that point.

Though I had worked closely with Anne Mulcahy to shepherd Xerox through a major financial crisis, it was much different being an actual CEO. I had never led a public company, especially one in which my family owned a 10 percent stake. My thirty-four-year-old niece, Meg, had just ten years of business experience and was already the company's president and COO. It was an experience similar to what Dick Lloyd had gone through when he took over Rutgers after Bill Foster left for Utah.

The difficulty was compounded by the fact that I didn't have the same intrinsic knowledge that my brother had had regarding how to make the company successful. He had always been the coach on the floor.

Brad did not have the money to pay highly experienced executives. So, he hired young employees and trained them. As a result, Medifast was filled with young people in key executive roles. When Brad was healthy, he could compensate and cover for his team like any good Marine did. But when he got sick and the company continued to grow, many in the management team still were learning on the job.

The younger executives were forced to take more responsibility, and they made short-sighted decisions in accounting and advertising. They were hardworking individuals who made decisions they thought were good, but they were made from a limited perspective. Some of these decisions also resulted in a federal investigation into the company's advertising. The stockholders also became concerned. The company faced lawsuits from them. This resulted in one of Medifast's subsidiaries, Jason Pharmaceuticals, Inc., paying a $3.7 million fine to the Treasury Department on behalf of the Federal Trade Commission regarding advertising violations without admission of fault. Medifast also agreed to pay a two-hundred-thousand-dollar civil penalty to the SEC in 2013 relating to an investigation into our financial reporting from 2006 to 2009.

There also needed to be changes in our distribution model. We had success using coaches, and it was great. But the coaches did not like the fact that customers could also order Medifast products directly from the internet. The coaches felt this caused confusion and limited their ability to be successful. Brad and I realized we had conflict in the company.

Two months before my brother passed away, I went to the board of directors and let them know that if I was going to be held responsible, I needed to be the CEO as well as chairman of the board.

They agreed.

Being a chairman of the board is different from being a CEO. Every other place I had been, a leader made the final decision. He or she got to select the team. At Medifast, I needed to lead by consensus. It was a little different "sell" than I had known at Xerox. Leading a board requires navigation. I had to manage people who had different agendas and were coming from different angles. I had to create a successful matrix. Some members I invited. Some I inherited. There is not a month that goes by when I don't talk to every member of the board, see how they're doing, how they feel. If I don't have good communication skills, I might get out of sync with them.

Early in this transition, I realized our senior management team had limited skills. I wanted to reach our goals, and we needed more experienced managers who could harness the abilities of our employees. This meant that there needed to be a changing of the guard in various positions. Many of the employees had not grown to meet Medifast's current needs.

We had a good product. The foundation was a little shaky. When I assumed the CEO role, I felt it was important to get a more credentialed CFO, because the SEC wasn't going to allow us to do business the way we had done it before. This allowed me to build a corporate governance structure essential to the company's success.

In addition to leadership, we also needed an infusion of operational talent.

I felt it necessary to bring trained individuals who had backgrounds with established companies—like Black & Decker, AT&T, and Avon— who would enhance the way the company did business. My niece Meg and the current employees understood the Medifast culture, but they were still learning on the job, as I mentioned. They needed to do things more effectively.

We filled out the starting lineup with Tim Robinson from Canon as our CFO. Brad had hired Brian Kagan in marketing, who was a hot commodity from Black & Decker. When Brad got sick, he brought in Jason Groves, who had been a board member, to become our general counsel.

We also needed leadership in the field. Realizing how much I had benefited from my experiences at Xerox, I went back to the well. Jeanne City, our Vice President, Human Resources, and I hired Dom Vietri to run our clinic business. Brian Lloyd, Dick Lloyd's nephew and a Brown graduate, worked on international partnerships. Art Fonari, who was a former football player from Marshall University and the head of the supply chain at Xerox, came in to help train my brother's son-in-law, Guy Sheetz, on the supply-chain business. I brought my old friend Ed Ciaschi back as a consultant. I also hired Valerie Blauvelt, my longtime marketing person, to create a long-term sales strategy. Jason worked on upgrading our legal team and settling the lawsuits.

It was an all-star team, much like I'd had at Xerox. But Brad and I had contrasting management styles. Though I shared Brad's vision for the company, we were very different people. Brad had much more of an entrepreneurial approach. He had a type A personality, with charisma, and knew how to rally his troops to a cause. My management style was more structured and process oriented. Medifast had become a much larger organization, in need of the kind of structure and process I could provide, to ensure sustainable growth.

My brother's DNA combined with his Marine training had allowed him to charge up any hill. He never led blindly. The only person he was afraid of was my mother. She'd say, "Jump." He'd ask, "How high?"

Brad also was a stickler for the rules. It was the yin and yang of why he was successful.

One of the things you're supposed to do in a public company is to send a notice out before a board meeting takes place. I screwed up and forgot to do it once. I walked into the hospital room to see Brad. He was as sick as a dog. But that did not stop him from jumping all over me. "Mike," he said. "Goddamn it, I'm not even going to the board meeting because you are such a jerk, you didn't send out a notice." Then he jumped on the phone with Jason and ripped into him, too. "You guys got to follow the right procedures," he said.

We still had the meeting.

That was my brother. I didn't feel so bad, though, after Meg related an experience she'd had with Brad. He'd fired her for a day for being five minutes late. His work was his life.

Medifast needed more structure, but I wasn't starting from scratch. Our teams, like those at Xerox, were empowered to make decisions. I was more cautious than Brad but similar to him; everyone was always held accountable. It reminded me of the basketball teams I had played on. Accountability was the number-one priority. What's most gratifying is when everyone understands the *why*. That's when the magic happens.

"If you are an entrepreneur, the risk is greater, because if you fail, you lose your house," Michael Shea once told me. You figure out very quickly what it is going to take to make it work. Michael was a friend who built a one-billion-dollar business at Global Images and sold it to Xerox. He also told me that I needed to create a culture shift. He understood that Medifast, like his company, needed a cohesive leadership team working together to grow the business.

I knew that to be successful, the company needed a more professional approach.

"Brad was exactly what the company needed when Medifast started," Jason recalls. "He was a risk taker. He was a gunslinger and a cowboy. I think of him fondly. He would use any means necessary to get things done. Mike and I were both on the board of directors. I first met Mike the day Brad called us in to tell us he was dying, in 2011. He asked me to come on as general counsel, and he asked Mike to come in as chairman. We quickly became fast friends. We both understood how big companies worked. He had been at Xerox, and I had been at Verizon for ten years.

"It was hard to imagine that departments didn't have budgets. They just had profits and losses. Mike was like, 'This can't be.' He implemented new checks and balances. This was particularly hard when Brad was alive, because it was not familiar to him or his employees, who pushed back. When Mike took control as CEO, he began crafting more systematic processes that enabled Medifast to reach more people. He used top-level consultants. He began running the company like a Fortune 500 corporation that was coming out of debt.

"Mike was the link between Brad, who had a bold vision of the company, and Dan Chard, our current CEO. Frankly, he was the only person who could have done it. The fact he was Brad's brother allowed him to empathetically and compassionately make the changes the company needed while preserving what Brad had built."

When I became CEO, we were in the middle of building our own com-pany-owned clinics—a strategy I quickly realized could turn disastrous. We had opened seventy clinics in less than twelve months. The numbers showed that this was not going to work. If we didn't call an audible, our profits could have taken a nine-million-dollar hit. I quickly decided to replace the rollout of company-owned clinics with a less capital-inten-sive model that would still enable Medifast to grow its clinic distribution channel but with less of a cash outlay. When I told Brad in February 2012, I did not know how he would take it. But I showed him the financials, and he said, "Do what you got to do."

At this time, I put together the company's first-ever five-year strategic plan. We held monthly strategy meetings and weekly staff sessions led by Meg's teams with help from Valerie Blauvelt.

Our team created the plan to drive revenue to a one-billion-dollar goal for the company.

Being a child of Xerox, I decided to invest in technology, as I wanted to increase online sales and improve distribution and manufacturing. The upgrades in the manufacturing plants allowed workers to crank out three to four times the previous annual volume, and the capacity for growth was in place. All the powder products were made at the Owing Mills plant. Other products were outsourced to partners. We launched twen-ty-five new products by 2014.

Like my parents, I put a lot of emphasis on education. I was looking to make the company more professional. Ed and I partnered with George-town University to create a leadership development program. We also did a similar program with Stevenson University, a small college in Owings Mills that provided management training opportunities for our incum-bent managers and management candidates. "We had several managers in Medifast who had never been to a formal management program," Ed says. "Both programs provided opportunities for learning and focused on the vision of Medifast that unified the headquarters groups to support the field coaches. The executive leadership program was held at the George-town campus for five days, while the attendees spent the evenings having dinner together and coming together as a team."

Brian Kagan says it was the first time the team had come together as a whole. "I believe the participation of the groups at headquarters and field teams was a turning point in the direction the company," he adds.

We started to see improvements in Medifast's revenues. By the end of 2012, they had jumped to a healthy $356.7 million, with annual earnings per share of $1.16. The stock went from fourteen dollars to twenty-eight dollars to thirty-two dollars, and there was room for growth internationally.

Things were going well. Our stockholders were happy. Then, on May 14, 2014, we noticed that Glenn Welling from Engaged Capital bought 6 percent of the stock. That set off alarm bells. To add fuel to the fire, on August 25, 2014, Warren Lichtenstein, a hedge fund owner, had bought nearly 10 percent of Medifast in one day through another company he owns, Modus Link Security Corp. Lichtenstein had been involved in over one hundred proxy fights. He acquired companies.

Lichtenstein's intent was to buy Medifast. We were doing our job well. But he realized he couldn't afford to buy us. It still worked out for him. Due to the stock price increasing, he walked away with a quick eight to ten million dollars.

Welling, on the other hand, wanted to flip the company like we were a property on the HGTV channel. He filed a Schedule 13D with the Securities and Exchange Commission, which allowed him, as an investor with over 5 percent of the shares in a publicly held company, to attempt a hostile takeover if he believed the stock was undervalued; or maybe he was contemplating a proxy fight with the goal of controlling the voting or replacing management.

Welling claimed that our stock was undervalued due to the negative publicity certain multilevel marketers got following another federal investigation.

Medifast stock had risen from thirteen dollars to thirty-two dollars a share, but Welling thought it should have been higher. He also claimed I wasn't the best person to run the company because of my lack of experience running a multilevel marketing company. He also thought my niece was in over her head. He did not like the fact that the MacDonald family had been running the company for so long. He wanted to see the company sold, and felt he could make a lot of money from the transaction. I still have a copy of the SEC filing in my briefcase as a reminder.

When he filed in court, our stock had gone up 265 percent in five years, and shares had gone from four dollars in 2009 to twenty-nine dollars in 2014.

Takeovers—in which one company makes an offer to assume control of another—are common in the business world. Larger companies tend to take over smaller ones if they want to get into a new market. When Medifast became the target of a hostile takeover, one of the things we did to fight off Welling was to utilize a poison-pill strategy, a defense tactic meant to discourage hostile takeover attempts. The strategy is based on the idea of something that is difficult to swallow or accept. "Poison pills" in terms in this case allow existing shareholders the right to purchase additional shares at a discounted rate. The greater the number of stockholders who buy additional shares, the more diluted the acquiring company's interest becomes. This makes the cost of the bid much higher.

We spent millions of dollars to fight off these people, but we had to do it to protect the other stockholders. During that time, Kevin Byrnes, the chair of our mergers and acquisitions committee, did an outstanding job working with consultants to defend the company against the activists. The board gave me outstanding support, and I had the guts to stand up to the activists. Welling came in and said, "Mike, you know nothing about consumer products and multilevel marketing." I had gone to our convention for years and years. I knew a lot about multilevel marketing. I had been on the board of the Direct Selling Association for five years with the heads of Mary Kay, USANA, and Nu Skin. But I still was willing to learn at an older age. That is an important message for anybody. I could manage anything. To me, it is a matter of applying leadership skills, good communication, and high ethical values.

In the process, the takeover activists also went after my niece.

Jeff Brown was on the board of directors at Medifast and was also on other boards with Welling. When Welling decides he wants a company, he tends to place Jeff on the board to assist him. I met him for dinner one night. Jeff said to me, "Why does your niece work for you?"

I said, "She's my niece, and she's doing a good job. There is no way I'm firing my niece. I understand there've been a lot of stories about family in this company, but this family built this company. There's going to be a point where the family is not going to lead the company, but it's going to be through evolution. I'm going to do it in a way that makes the company successful going forward, but it will be a company decision."

We walked out of the dinner with a mutual respect. I appreciated his candor, and I'd like to believe he felt our company was successful. Meg was part of that success. Changes would be made on our clock, not his.

The newfound respect didn't relieve the stress over the next six months. I had another outbreak of acid reflux. Jason took me to Hopkins, and my son-in-law, Anthony, stayed overnight with me.

We were working so much. I'd be on the phone with advisors until midnight, and Jason would still be working in the office. We were working twelve to fifteen hours a day. I was glad I wasn't paying Jason by the hour. We spent so much time together.

"It wasn't easy to manage the anxiety that Welling's attempted activist attack caused our company," Jason recalls. "It created a lot of disruption to our focus. It did not disrupt our business. Mike was determined to keep the business going," he says of my strategy. "He compartmentalized these issues with outside counsel and the consultants. He allowed the executives to run the day-to-day business. It was difficult. We had been through a lot—SEC investigations, class actions, shareholder lawsuits—but this [takeover attempt] by any measure presented the most challenges. We had all our chips on the table, and they knew it. Mike bet the whole company. Everything could be lost. It was for all the marbles. Mike had a very steady hand, a plan, and the ability to take us where we needed to go. He was unwilling to compromise if we didn't need to but was willing to compromise for success. His leadership saved the company. I question whether anyone else could have led the company through this time."

During our negotiations, I felt that Warren Lichtenstein was very fair. He came in and met with the company. He thought I was doing a good job with the company and said he could support me if I provided Glenn Welling the number of seats he required on the board. When my brother started the company, he did not offer much pay for a board seat, and he put a bunch of his friends on the board.

I agreed that corporate governance needed to change. That meant changing the composition of the board; there were ten board members at the time. Welling and I were on the board. I agreed to accept others that he and I supported. But I kept six people, because I needed to maintain a majority if I wanted to stay in power. I can't believe that less than a year later, our stock prices had increased, and I remained the CEO after two activists had attacked our company. Welling eventually sold his position in 2016.

Though I'd never want to go through it again, Welling's involvement helped us restructure the board and helped us with capital reallocation. The problem was, he made it personal. He didn't realize that Brad and I had brought so many people into the business. We had known people like Wayne Andersen and Dan Bell for over ten years. When you bring in the new, you don't have to throw out the old. There are certain things that can't be traded on the floor of the New York Stock Exchange. This kind of appreciation for the people at Medifast is exactly like what I'd had for every teammate who'd played with me on the basketball court.

CHAPTER 12

The OPTAVIA Turnaround

Through all the many challenges that Medifast dealt with during my tenure, revenue for 2014 was $285 million and the market cap fluctuated between $330 million and $400 million. We had a great product. We were continuing to improve how we were conducting business.

Now, we needed to find a way to expand our reach.

What continued to make our company great is that everyone involved shared a vision that it would reach a worth of over one billion dollars.

Our revenues were based on a two percent share of the weight-loss industry. Obesity is a major issue in this country. We were quickly being recognized as a solution to this problem.

While still the CEO, I was able to visualize new opportunities with many on the team, including my niece Meg and Dr. A. Drawing on my multinational experience from Xerox, I believed we could duplicate our success in other countries. We began working with a weight-loss company called Medex in Mexico. It had a business model similar to ours. We began to distribute our product through Medex's network of clinics. Though I was certain there was a need for Medifast outside the United States, I was reminded that it was important to understand each market. The product was set at the wrong price. There was little traction in the market. We were unsuccessful in part because although we believed in our product, we needed to focus on the sales process to have a broader sales appeal in Hong Kong, Singapore, France, or the United States.

We all agreed that the name OPTAVIA was perfect. It was a simple concept that was understood in all languages.

We had the luxury of having Dr. A on our team. His *New York Times* bestseller, *Dr. A's Habits of Health*, was an immediate touchstone for all interested in weight loss. He had always been keen on taking Take Shape for Life from product sales to being a lifestyle transformation company. He created the clay as well as the models by which customers would eat healthy food, lose weight, and maintain an optimal weight one healthy habit at a time. If instead of being taught how to go on a diet, clients are taught a set of healthy habits for a lifetime, that makes all the difference for their continuing success.

Dr. A saw the OPTAVIA products as the ingredients, or "fuelings," that could be available in kits or as individual items, ranging from full meals to light snacks. The full line was separated into two categories—essential and select. OPTAVIA products were available only through independent coaches, who each had their own replicated websites and gave customers support, encouragement, and accountability beyond the products they purchased. As clients experienced positive results—whether it was weight loss or an increase in energy—it was hoped they would become coaches themselves, growing the network.

OPTAVIA coaches made the difference—they made it possible to separate OPTAVIA from the competition, because they focused on individual transformation.

It was a sound idea.

Like all good ideas, it needed the proper merchandising, marketing, and distribution.

Many of our answers were found when we hired Mona Ameli as the president of Take Shape for Life, Medifast's direct-sales division.

Mona had a tremendous amount of expertise and a unique background that qualified her for the challenge. She was a Middle Easterner who had been educated in Paris before she immigrated to the United States after college. When she arrived in the U.S., she was in her mid-twenties and had a limited command of the English language. She did not even know how to drive and had to claw her way up the corporate ladder as a woman, a minority, and a foreigner.

But she has become one of the best in the profession. Her skills were matched by her interest in nutrition companies. I had a great appreciation for her abilities as she spent time on every step of the corporate ladder. She had worked for Shaklee Corporation, Natural Alternatives International and Herbalife International. She had served as general manager of Peru-based Belcorp, the world's ninth-largest direct-selling company, where she led the U.S. beauty and lifestyle products business.

This was going to be another Jeff Ruland recruiting scenario.

We weren't the only people knocking on her door. Mona was recognized as one of the twenty most influential women in the direct-sales industry. She also was considered one of the most powerful and influential women by the National Diversity Council. I felt a kindred spirit with her personally because she was a coach at heart. She worked to help other women succeed. From 2007 to 2011, she ran Women Without Borders, a nonprofit group she founded to help victims of domestic abuse.

We were looking for someone to manage the biggest piece of our business at Medifast. OPTAVIA accounted for 70 percent of our company's sales through an inspired independent group of coaches. We had 9,300 coaches in our network. And the team needed someone to double that number and take it international. She had proven she could do this with her previous employers.

When Mona was considering the job, she was intrigued. Medifast was bringing in two hundred million dollars with the number of coaches we had. We were lucky we were singing from the same hymnal, as she too saw the same potential. Mona not only realized the opportunity but also understood the need to shift focus so the company could grow. She helped with the strategy and rollout of OPTAVIA. "It was really important that we build a brand that could have a global appeal," she says. "Most of my experiences were global, and Take Shape for Life did not resonate around the globe. Using an idiom like OPTAVIA was, as the word implies, the optimal way."

When we began working, Mona jumped in quickly. It was one of the reasons Medifast was successful.

She understood, like all of us, that this new line of products—including bars, crackers, and shakes—reflected the essence of the OPTAVIA brand. OPTAVIA was going to add probiotics and other nutrients that were just as important. These products would be sold exclusively through our OPTAVIA network. To ensure worldwide appeal, we engaged Helen Irwin from England, who ran a branding company, and made her responsible for the rebranding and repackaging of the product for global distribution.

We knew it would take a while for OPTAVIA to gain customer loyalty. The experience for me was similar experience to being president of global marketing my last few years at Xerox. It was important that the Xerox logo be modern and recognizable in the digital world. So the company moved to a lowercase treatment of the Xerox name—in a vibrant red— along with a spherical symbol sketched with lines that link to form an illustrated "X," representing Xerox's connections to its customers, partners, industry, and innovation. The new logo also was designed to be more effectively animated for use on multimedia platforms.

It sounds simple. But it's a major undertaking. When we decided to rebrand our image at Medifast, that meant changing everything from the business cards and the stationery to the logo and the launch of the product. At a company like Xerox, rebranding cost hundreds of millions of dollars.

It's also a very risky business.

I thought it was a needed next step at Medifast to make sure we didn't lose our existing customers. Take Shape for Life had been around for twelve years.

With the risks there is always the possibility of a reward. At the first Medifast national convention, only twenty people came to our factory outside Baltimore.

In 2016, there were over 3,400 registered attendees for that year's convention at the Gaylord Texan Hotel and Convention Center in

Grapevine, Texas. The enthusiasm when Dr. A announced the unveiling of the OPTAVIA product line was overwhelming. This meal-delivery diet program that engaged our growing network to help people make healthier choices was easily understood by the then 12,800 coaches. Mona and I were onstage with Dr. A. It was total excitement. I had never seen anything like it at one of our conventions. For a moment, I felt like I was back in the Barn during my college days. This was also a wonderful time to meet everyone in the Medifast family who contributed to our success. Jean and I enjoyed going every year and were always energized by the passion and professionalism of the Medifast network. One of the most rewarding parts was that the coaches were as concerned with me as they were with their own customers. If they saw I had gained a few pounds, they would be all over me. They were committed to the idea that everyone should be living a healthy lifestyle.

When I saw clients who had lost fifty to a hundred pounds, it was a lot more satisfying than selling a new copier. I met one lady who claimed she had lost five hundred pounds over a six-year period. I don't know. But people who do very well on our program love to show their before-and-after pictures. I always felt that what my brother did helped a lot of people. Medifast is not some fly-by-night company. It has become a huge success story, and it took years to build.

The company booths were packed in 2016, selling Medifast products and newly packaged OPTAVIA samples. There were also self-help books from Dr. A and T-shirts promoting OPTAVIA. The coaches' commitment to Medifast, combined with their recognition that OPTAVIA would be accepted worldwide, allowed our company to clear one bar and raise another.

Each day, there was a crescendo of enthusiasm when Dr. A explained that the OPTAVIA products made the difference for customers in the network. It was gratifying to me when customers told their personal stories about why they had lost weight and joined as coaches. The direct sales allowed health care professionals to become partners. They weren't competing against brick-and-mortar company stores and clinics. They were using Medifast as part of a plan to help people, and they gained control over the new products by distributing them through their websites.

We needed to capitalize on the momentum.

When I agreed to join the company, I was getting close to sixty-five. Now I needed to step aside. I felt good that we had professionalized the organization, created more of a corporate culture, and brought in a woman who was an expert in direct selling. But now we needed the final piece of the puzzle.

It was important to everyone that I was part of the search for my replacement. Under the observation of many, the search committee settled on Dan Chard, a twenty-five-year veteran of the direct-sales and consumer-products industry. He was an expert in multilevel marketing and had spent eight years with General Mills. He had served seventeen years with Nu Skin, where he had been president of global sales. I agreed to stay on for a year in my role as chairman of the board to help with the transition, and I still serve on the board as a chairman in a nonexecutive capacity today.

Dan was a rising star who had a proven track record of taking businesses to the next level. He had been well-educated at Brigham Young University and gotten his master's degree from University of Minnesota. It was evident every time we dealt with him that he possessed high moral and ethical values. He had a strong background in international finance. He'd originally worked with Arthur Andersen's tax division in Hong Kong, and I thought his brain could take us to the next level.

We had to convince him that Medifast was a good next step.

"I was hesitant at the beginning, because I didn't want to get into the weight-management space and I was worried about the kind of people who would be involved in that kind of company," Dan says. "I wanted to make sure the company would take me to the end of my career. I wanted to make sure it was something I believed in. I was interested enough to say I'd love to meet the CEO, Mike MacDonald, and see where it went. I met Mike for breakfast in New York, and what I found was a man who was very principled, with high moral character. He told me about his brother Brad. He shared similar values of faith. He and his family are extremely involved in the Catholic Church. I was touched when he told me the story of quitting a good job in Chicago to come here because he wanted to keep his brother's legacy alive. I went through something similar when I left a promising job to take care of my mother in Salt Lake City. I found myself feeling he was someone who would be involved in something that was good. When I say 'good,' I wanted something that was going to be meaningful in a variety of ways."

The next day Dan flew to Baltimore to meet with Dr. A, Mona, and our CFO, Tim Robinson. Then he attended our convention with his wife to meet with some of our coaches, who were the biggest part of the division. "My wife is a great judge of character," Dan says, "and we came away impressed with the foundation Brad and Mike had built and the good people who were involved."

When he came aboard in the fourth quarter of 2016, he got right to work. He was as busy as the bees in the hive that appears on the state flag of Utah. One of the things we did was simplify the distribution of the Medifast products. When my brother built the company, he had four distribution channels. The original channels set up by Brad had run their course. The company-owned clinics were less profitable. Our franchise clinics were successful. We weren't advertising heavily on the internet. As in any organization, people were important, and our coaches were our people.

I didn't want to put all our eggs in one basket. My Xerox experience told me not to give up on the internet completely. Dan was a big proponent of the coaches. He explained to me why they were the only way to go. We made the decision that our primary involvement with direct selling would be with OPTAVIA with some internet support. It was the first time in the history of Medifast that management was on common ground with every employee.

As much as I wanted to leave, I continued to be excited about the opportunities. I knew we were going to become a one-billion-dollar company. In many ways, it was back to the future—reminding me of Xerox. All the leaders went into the field, and Mona stayed with the team at headquarters. Everyone knew their role. Dr. A was the spokesperson.

Then Mona would capture the message, and Helen would reinforce the power of the products. Our network of coaches would reiterate the value of a better lifestyle.

Dan's greatest contribution not only was helping launch OPTAVIA in 2017; he also implemented a strategy to increase our network. We've gone from 12,500 to 36,500 coaches, adding 20,000 in the past four years alone. Many have invested themselves by going through a certification process, and have agreed not to compromise the equity we've built. This way, everyone can have success. They are motivated because they can work full- or part-time. They can coach on FaceTime. Anytime you are helping someone else, it makes you feel good. The product sells itself.

Our success illustrates the appeal of OPTAVIA. The numbers have been eye-popping.

"Our run has been going on for a while," Dan says. "In 2018, we were up 66 percent. In 2019, we were up 42 percent. It's really a reflection of Medifast being relevant for the times, where people are very focused on health and wellness. We're helping people who have failed on diets. We're establishing a set of healthy habits. The first habit they learn is healthy eating. And through reinforcing those habits, they may achieve a lifestyle change that could take them through the rest of their lives."

There still is room for growth.

The company's corporate headquarters have moved to the Harbor East in Baltimore to keep current and attract new talent. This has proven to be productive.

Dan hired Nick Johnson as president of OPTAVIA. His current title is president of coach and client experience. He had big shoes to fill after Mona left. Nick, who was named one of Direct Selling News' "Forces Under 40" in 2017, brought more than ten years of experience in direct selling, marketing, and client relations as vice president of sales and marketing for Nu Skin Enterprises. He had overseen sales and marketing in twenty-seven countries, including areas in the Middle East, Europe, and Africa. He is in charge of expansion into Singapore and Hong Kong. We opened our first offices there in 2019.

Medifast has evolved into a multinational company. A recent high-water mark for OPTAVIA was when the senior leadership staff gathered on the iconic platform at the New York Stock Exchange to ring the market's opening bell in early March 2020. This opportunity was a credit to the independent OPTAVIA coaches responsible for the brand's incredible success. The stock went from $3.52 in 2008 to as high as $207 in 2020—just twelve years. The company revenue went from fifteen million dollars the year my brother became the CEO to over seven hundred million today.

We were planning another big event for July 2020. We rented an arena in Atlanta for our company's annual convention, which was expected to be the biggest ever. But the traditional in-person event was canceled due to the global coronavirus pandemic. The presentation has already been viewed by over 140,000 people on Facebook. Many of the coaches hosted watch parties and engaged with their peers through social media.

For my entire business career, I have been part of either Xerox or Medifast. The companies have been an extension of my family. I still believe, as I did when I put on my Saint Laurence uniform, that your teammates matter the most. I've also always known that someone else can take your place in the lineup. My mom and dad showed me that no matter what your job is, your responsibility is to perform at your best every second you are there. The role of every CEO is to treat people right, create a good environment, and make it work. Someday someone will replace you.

If they're good, they'll do it well.

CHAPTER 13

Giving Back

Throughout my career, whether in business or basketball, I was able to enjoy success through great teachers, hard work, and a little luck. With only twenty-four hours in the day and seven days in the week, too often people don't make time to help others from an outside organization or team.

I was invited to join the board of directors on the V Foundation for Cancer Research in 1994, when I was a vice president at Xerox. I got a call from Pam Valvano, who said to me, "Mike, you have a relationship with our family, and we're looking for businesspeople to help run the board and start raising money. We already have enough celebrities."

Often, we've been able to raise the bottom line.

Everyone knows someone who has dealt with this disease. I have lost a sister, Florence, and a brother, Brad, to cancer. Having Jim Valvano's passion for basketball and life, I wanted to share in the responsibility. And this time, as with any time Jim asked me, I couldn't say no.

When Jim made his unexpected trip to Reynolds Coliseum on the campus of North Carolina State on February 21, 1992, to celebrate the tenth anniversary of the Wolfpack's Cinderella run to the NCAA tournament championship, he was a different person than he had been in 1983 and a much different person than I remember working for at Iona.

Jim was such a ball of energy that special night, running around the court at the Pit looking for someone to hug in the thrill of victory after Lorenzo Charles's tip-in gave the Wolfpack a 54–52 victory over heavily favored Houston.

But it was also clear that the years had taken their toll on him, beginning in 1989, when he was dismissed from his jobs as athletic director and head basketball coach at NC State in the wake of a wide-ranging scandal. He also had been diagnosed with an aggressive form of glandular cancer that was attacking his bones. He was still working for ESPN in 1992 and was scheduled to do commentary for ABC TV on the Wolfpack's ACC game against Duke. But he had missed his previous assignment, and no one knew if he would be physically capable of showing up. ABC had already booked former NC State player Terry Gannon as a stand-in.

But Jim did not want to miss this. When he made his way into the building, he was bent over and struggling to walk. But he made it to center court for the pre-game ceremony, greeting his ex-players and then addressing the Wolfpack faithful for the last time, talking openly about the fight of his life.

"Cancer can't rob me of my heart, my mind, or my soul," he said.

Then he borrowed a line from the great British prime minister Winston Churchill in World War II. "Don't ever, ever give up," he said. Then he sang the Wolfpack fight song, leading the fans just as Arthur Fiedler had led the Boston Pops.

When Jim finished, there wasn't a dry eye in the crowd. People were as mesmerized by him as they had been during his tenure at Raleigh.

"When I saw him, I was like, 'Oh wow, he's really sick.' But we all thought he would beat it," says Derek Whittenburg, who led the 1983 team onto the court and now has become the de facto spokesman for the championship team. "We never thought it was going to end. I called him a couple times, but I couldn't bring myself to go to the hospital. I wanted to remember him just as he was when he was coaching us."

Jim was dying. The doctors knew it. Jim was hoping for another miracle like the one he had gotten in the 1983 title game.

But he never got it.

Nine days after the reunion, Jim traveled to New York City to accept the Arthur Ashe Courage Award at the first-ever ESPY Awards. He gave one of the most inspirational speeches ever. There is no doubt that he channeled his inner Vince Lombardi. It still tugs on everyone's heart strings today.

But Jim almost didn't make the nationally televised prime-time event. Pam had to help him into his tuxedo. He developed severe chills and was huddled on the bed in his hotel room shivering prior to the event. He had lost thirty-five pounds, could hardly walk, and had no sense of taste. When his colleague John Saunders visited him, he realized that given Jim's condition, Jim shouldn't attend.

But the opportunity was too important for Jim not to share his story.

When he arrived at Radio City Music Hall, he was racked with pain. Duke's Mike Krzyzewski and Hall of Fame broadcaster Dick Vitale had to help him to the stage. But once he stood behind the podium and the TV lights came on, it energized him like no one could have imagined. And, as he always did, he garnered everyone's attention.

It was like he had been transported back to the metro coaches' luncheons, where he had told jokes that would have made Henny Youngman take notes. He talked about his family and his own journey. He also provided a little sage advice for everyone.

"I believe you should do three things every single day of your life," he said. "One, you should laugh. Two, you should think. Pause and think about your life. And three, you should cry. Get yourself into a state of emotion where you shed a tear. If you do all three of those things—laugh, think, and cry—well, that's a heck of a day. If you do those things for a week, it's something special."

Eight minutes into his speech, Jim saw "thirty seconds" flashing at him on the teleprompter. "Hey, look at that," he said. "Thirty seconds. Some guy is telling me I've got thirty seconds left. You think I care about some guy telling me I've got thirty seconds left? I've got tumors all over my body, and I'm supposed to care about a guy telling me I've got thirty seconds?

"Freak you," he said in colorful Italian.

Before he left the stage, Jim announced he was launching the V Foundation for Cancer Research in conjunction with ESPN. "Our motto will be, 'Don't give up. Don't ever give up.' It may not save my life, but it may save my children's lives."

He received the final standing ovation of his life.

Before that night, he and his wife Pam had met with ESPN president Steve Bornstein of to discuss the idea. He had written on a legal pad a list of the members of the first board of directors. They included Steve, Pam, Nick Valvano, Bob Valvano, former college roommate Bob Lloyd, Derek, John Saunders of ESPN, Krzyzewski, Dick, Dr. Joseph Moore (his primary oncologist), and Dr. Robert Bass; both doctors were from Duke University Medical Center.

Two weeks later, Jim died at age forty-seven.

Nick, who had always been amazed by his brother's talent, accomplishments, and vision, is still processing twenty-eight years later how he underestimated his brother.

"It was one of the most touching speeches ever made by anybody," he says. "And I missed it. I was with Jim two days earlier in the hospital, and we're sitting talking and I ask him, 'Tell me about the thing you're going to do. I'm supposed to be in Chicago for a big meeting.' He says to me, 'Oh, nah. Don't change your plans. This is the first year they're having it.' How's that for a bad decision?

"The pain is there after all these years. It's so nice when people tell me stories about him, but it emotionally wears me out.

"I got a letter recently from a girl who was about eight or nine years old from New Jersey. She said, 'My dad made me watch the speech from your brother, and he reminds me of my grandfather when he was dying from cancer. I just wanted to tell you how much I enjoyed Jim's speech.'

"The family owns a printing company. I called her father up and asked, 'Do you know how special your daughter is?' I'm crying, and I say, 'I've got to meet you.' So, we invited them down to the Jimmy V. Women's

Classic in Raleigh with Connecticut, NC State, Tennessee, and Duke. I introduced them to the coaches, and the kid was in heaven."

Heaven isn't just about cutting down the nets.

"Jimmy V's legacy will not be cutting the nets down in the national championship," Dick says. "The bottom line: He will impact people for years and years and years. Think of it. He died in 1993. Since then, a quarter of a billion dollars has been raised in his name for cancer research."

I was so far removed. Putting myself into my work and raising my family, I didn't make time for anything else. Embarrassingly, I didn't realize the impact he'd had, and was still having, but I shouldn't have been surprised. This was a "Jimmy V. special."

The commitment of the entire board is phenomenal.

"The first thing you need to know from my perspective: I am a four-time cancer survivor," says Harry Rhoads, a senior partner in the Washington Speakers Bureau and a member of the board. "In 1988, I went to see a dermatologist. He saw a spot on my back and wanted to get it removed. When I was coming out of surgery, my phone rang, and it was Jim Valvano. He was the first person to call me after I got treatment. He was right in the middle of practice. He's talking to me, blowing the whistle and giving me advice. We had a great conversation although I was pretty drugged up. A couple years later, I had a little weekend place and the phone rings, and it's Jim telling me he's just been diagnosed with cancer. I was just shattered by the news. When my partner and I started the program [Washington Speakers Bureau], it was 1980, and Jim signed with us in 1984. He was one of my earliest friends, and then the news came.

"I got a call from Steve Bornstein telling me about the foundation. Jim had asked me to serve on the board. I had no idea what to expect. Of course, he was well-intentioned, but I didn't know who was going to be on the board. I didn't know anyone. During our first couple meetings, I met a group of amazing people, like George Bodenheimer, the former president of ESPN and one of the most revered figures in sports.

"The essence of leadership comes down to two words—decision making. You got to know when to pull the trigger. I met Coach K [Duke head coach Mike Krzyzewski]; met Dr. Joe Moore, who was Jim's doctor at Duke Medical Center. Sixteen years later, when my cancer came back, the first thing I did was go down to Duke and see Joe Moore. I had three or four bouts with cancer, and I got all my treatment at Duke."

Steve Bornstein was the founder of the V Foundation. Then Nick Valvano joined to continue his brother's legacy as CEO. We knew each other from Jim's basketball camps, and he was also on the team at Xerox. I told Pam I would be happy to join the board. I've been a willing member for the past twenty-seven years.

Not only does the board raise incredible amounts of money, but every dollar goes to research. This is possible because the board subsidizes everything. It's important that we pay for everything. Contributions by members are never solicited; they are given willingly because we all want to ensure the success of the foundation.

Every team needs a great backcourt. The V Foundation is led by Bob Lloyd and Nick. With Rutgers it was Bob and Jim; this time it's Bob and Nick. I can only begin to imagine what it's like to be in Nick's shoes. I imagine it's like my experience at Medifast when my brother Brad died from cancer and I took over as CEO. Nick was running a foundation for his brother because family was involved.

After Bob and Nick stepped down, the leadership transitioned to Steve Bornstein and George Bodenheimer. George was charged with fundraising and determined where the money could be best used. He was fortunate to have a group of top cancer researchers in the country to assist him.

"The V Foundation is so firmly embedded in the culture of ESPN," George says. "The two organizations are intertwined. It's such a blessing to have the foundation associated with the company, because so many employees want to give back. It's a mutually beneficial love affair. I've been heading up this two-hundred-million-dollar capital campaign, so I've been talking with a lot of donors over the last seven years. The fact the money is going to research is such a strong selling point.

"I did not know Jim that well when he worked for ESPN. I was a middle-level guy in the sales department. I just watched the speech recently.

My wife and I were in the audience that night. At the time, I didn't realize the impact it would have."

Most of the first board members were involved in basketball or had a personal connection with Jim. The opportunity to be part of such a selfless group and learn from them helped me when I became president of Xerox. I was doing things for the right reasons. They always asked how they could help. They weren't looking for anything in return. What a great lesson. It really reminded me to think before I acted. My board membership also allowed me to observe why so many basketball coaches and executives are successful. I got to work with Mike Krzyzewski, who was a role model. I remember watching him play and coach when he was at West Point. I was working as a scout for Jimmy at Iona. In scouting you can diagram the plays Mike runs. But working with him up close in the V Foundation was different. His ability to lead is humbling.

Nick came at it from a business background. Susan Braun, the current CEO, was previously the chair of the American Cancer Society's board. She approached her work on the board from a medical background. She and Nick had different approaches, but they were equally successful. The board meets four times a year, and the adage is true: The more you give, the more you get. Some of the events we planned were Dick Vitale's gala for pediatric cancer, a wine event in Napa, and a dinner hosted by Robin Roberts, former sportscaster on ESPN and current anchor of ABC's Good Morning America, in New York City.

The V Foundation became an extended family. It was my philanthropic priority.

I have supported things that have had an impact on my life, like the V Foundation, Rutgers University, and the Augustinian Order.

Bonner, though now run by the Archdiocese of Philadelphia, was in my time staffed by the Augustinian priests, who also run Villanova University. I soon realized it was important to get personally involved in Bonner because it had been a big part of my life. When the school opened in 1953, it had an enrollment of three thousand boys. Currently, it's about a third of that.

In 2005, the archdiocese announced that Bonner and its sister school, Archbishop Prendergast, for girls, would be consolidated into one high school. Seven years later, in 2012, the Augustinian friars withdrew from campus, citing a diminishing number of priests in the order. Based on the recommendations of a blue ribbon commission, Archbishop Charles Chaput announced that Bonner/Prendergast would be closing that June. Soon after the announcement, the school community began an appeals process to reverse the decision, which gained overwhelming support from the students, parents, and alumni. Days before the final decision, local businesspeople came forward with a plan to save all the high schools slated to close. Bonner was saved.

It is hard to imagine what my life would be like now if Bonner had not been accessible when I was in high school. The educational opportunities it provides, allowing low- to middle-class kids to dream about college, are invaluable. The school takes kids from one end of the spectrum to the other. Since both Brad's and my time at Bonner, the Augustinians have always been part of our families' lives. Brad even considered joining them as a vocation. Brad was not a great student in high school, but he was fairly religious. Father Melton from the guidance office guided him to follow his faith to the seminary. He spent one year at boarding school at Augustine's Academy on Long Island and then matriculated at Villanova. He lived in Mary's Hall with other seminarians. He made the dean's list. Just before he was scheduled to take his final vows,. he and two friends decided not to become priests, but they still earned their college degrees. During that time, Brad joined the ROTC, which paid his final two years of tuition. He also hustled other part-time jobs for money, just as my dad had done. My parents were still barely getting by on their own. Once we were eighteen in my family, we were expected to help out with family finances.

Brad still maintained a wonderful relationship with Father Melton later on. A former Marine Corps chaplain, Father Melton encouraged Brad to enlist in that branch of the service. Brad enjoyed every moment of it. He spent twenty-seven years as a Marine, rising to the rank of colonel before he was discharged, as I mentioned. And as you also now know, he then became successful in private business. After Brad died, Bonner was doing renovations. It seemed only appropriate that our family pay for a new guidance office with Brad's name on it.

Cancer is a terrible disease. After Brad died, my sister Florence was diagnosed with breast cancer, lung cancer, and brain cancer. She fought it for five years. I stopped in to see her in hospice at Misericordia Hospital in the Philadelphia suburbs the day she died. It has strengthened my resolve with the V Foundation.

If Bonner lit a fire under Brad and me, Rutgers added the gasoline and expanded my world. The relationships I made while being part of the Rutgers basketball team were enormously important to me. I felt a responsibility to support all the coaches because they supported me. I am hopeful the money I've contributed to a modern practice facility across from the RAC will help the program grow. It's wonderful that Jean's name and my name are on the conference rooms for men's and women's basketball. The film room is named after Jean's mom and dad, Ed and Honora Murock.

It is so rewarding to see the progress the Scarlet Knights have made since they hired Steve Pikiell as head coach in 2016. I stopped by his office not long after he got the job.

"Quite honestly, I didn't know who he was," Steve says of me on that visit. "We probably talked for an hour. He was so generous helping us financially, but what I like about him the most is, he will spend time with our players. Sometimes you just need former players like Mike to talk about Rutgers and how it contributed to their success in the business field, because 90 percent of them aren't going to play after college. He'll reach out to our point guard Geo Baker after a good game. Nick Brooks is one of our walk-ons, and he's kept in touch with him. I love that."

Rutgers has not been to the NCAA tournament since 1991. Can it be that long? And the team was going nowhere when Pikiell came on board four years ago after leading Stony Brook University to four American East championships and one NCAA appearance in ten years. "When I took this job, I knew the challenges. Rutgers had gone through five coaches in twelve years," Steve says. "They were in their fourth conference in eleven years, and we were on our fourth AD in seven years. In this new college atmosphere, everybody wants to know what's behind door number two.

"I learned my basketball from Jim Calhoun at Connecticut, who took a program that was playing in the eight-nine game at the Big East tournament and coached the school to three national championships. UConn had one coaching change and one league change in twenty-five years. Just one change and it's hard. When I was thinking about the job at Rutgers, I'm saying to myself, 'Can anybody succeed here?'"

It was probably the same question the previous four coaches had asked when they took the job.

"Everyone kept telling me Rutgers is where coaches go to die," Steve says. "Coach Calhoun was the one guy who told me it was worth a look. He could never understand why Rutgers couldn't be good. The other part of it was, I was looking for a new challenge. I could have probably stayed at Stony Brook for the rest of my career. It was a beautiful place to live, and the president Sam Stanley and I were really close. But I felt I had done everything I could do at Stony Brook University. So, it was good timing."

Steve is cut from the same cloth as Joe Boylan and Dick Vitale. He is very positive with the kids.

He is rebuilding a stagnant program from scratch, enabling the team to compete in the Big Ten—an idea that former president Ed Bloustein had planted in my head many years ago. Steve put the Scarlet Knights—a team with undervalued but developing players Geo Baker, wing Ron Harper Jr., and six-foot-ten center Myles Johnson—in position to have their name called on "Selection Sunday" in March 2020 after he had coached Rutgers to twenty wins, including a huge nonleague blowout of state rival Seton Hall at the RAC. The Scarlet Knights had eleven wins in league play against competition like nationally ranked Maryland. They even spent time in the AP Top Twenty-Five. They did it without any NBA players on the roster. No one averaged more than thirteen points. But the Knights won with depth, constantly aggressive defense, and rebounding. They were considered a lock to make the NCAA bracket after they defeated Purdue on the road in the final game of the regular season. The RAC was rocking a lot like the Barn had been back in my day.

But the NCAA games didn't happen, because of COVID-19.

"One thing about Rutgers: Their fans have been loyal for a long time," Steve says. "And now we've gotten the students as involved as they were in 1976."

CHAPTER 14

Family Values

From the bench to the boardroom, the journey has been filled with many experiences. Many mementos are on display in the library at my home. My parents imparted a love of learning, so my library always has been a special place for me. When entering this room, I am always reminded of the things that are important to me.

My favorite president is Abraham Lincoln. I have a reverence for his work to preserve the Union. I have a painting of Lincoln hanging behind my desk that was done by Steve Penley, a Georgia artist known for his love of statesmen. I also collect Remington statues, in honor of my grandfather, who was a member of the Seventh Cavalry in Arizona before becoming a world-famous surgeon in World War I.

I cherish the photographs of my mom and dad and of Jean and her family. I always chuckle when I see the picture of me with my brothers Brad and Bob at the Phoenix Open. It's hard to imagine that three brothers from Upper Darby would be hanging out with Tiger Woods, the Masters champion. There is a collage of pictures from my playing days at Rutgers, which quickly calls to mind the many lessons I learned from my teammates and from inspirational coaches like Bill Foster, Dick Lloyd, and Tom Young.

The room is filled with pictures of the Beatles and Elvis and auto-graphed guitars from Bruce Springsteen and Paul McCartney. I also have four autographed basketballs that remind me of the sport I enjoyed so much. Two are signed by Mike Krzyzewski and Dick Vitale and bring back memories of Jim Valvano. The other two are from current Rutgers men's and women's basketball coaches Steve Pikiell and Vivian Stringer, who are preserving the legacy of the programs.

These are important mementos. But the most meaningful thing to me is our family.

Family values were instilled by my parents and Jean's parents when she and I were growing up. No matter where work took me, I've tried to set an example for our children.

When Jean and I were married in 1977, we didn't have a crystal ball, but we did have a plan. We are fortunate to have three wonderful children—Ryan, forty-one; Stacey, thirty-nine; and Chris, thirty-three—and five wonderful grandchildren. I've been fortunate that I never needed Clarence from *It's a Wonderful Life* to remind me how lucky I am. Jean and I are proud of our children. We want them to feel like they can be themselves with us.

Rutgers is a big part of our extended family. Everyone wears Rutgers gear. I am ecumenical. I wear sweatshirts from Duke, NC State, Notre Dame, and Villanova because of my friendships and respect for the coaches and the former players I know from there.

Ryan followed my footsteps and graduated from Rutgers. He met his wife, Lauren, in class there. As a child, Jean used to tag along with her parents, who used to attend Rutgers football games and tailgate with their friends. Stacey started at Rutgers before transferring back home to Saint John Fisher College, a small Catholic college in suburban Rochester. She eventually married Anthony Cali, another Rutgers alum who is a former all-state quarterback and was the captain of the special teams on the 2006 nationally ranked football team.

I served on the Rutgers board of trustees for ten years and got to know two presidents—Edward Bloustein and Fran Lawrence—well. Fran was a huge baseball fan. When I was at Xerox, I still remember taking him to the all-star game in Boston. He was so excited because he loved the Red Sox. It was the night Ted Williams made the famous ride around Fenway Park when Major League Baseball recognized the top fifty players of the century. Fran and Ed were both great role models for me. Their leadership style was grounded in their personal ethics. I have fond memories of my time at the school.

When I played at Rutgers, I once had twenty relatives show up for one of my freshman games. My mom and dad came to most of my home games at the Barn, and Jean's parents were there as well. Once Rutgers started to climb into the AP Top Twenty-Five, tickets were hard to get, but our families had the right connection. Jean had access to two tickets, and I got two as a member of the team. The players always wanted more. "Whenever we had a big game, I don't know how many times I had to walk down to the ticket office," Jean says.

Those were the days.

I'm not around campus as much as I used to be. At sixty-seven, I am retired now and split time between my home overlooking the Manasquan River in New Jersey and my home in Palm Beach Gardens, Florida. Perhaps it's in the MacDonald family genes to be constantly moving. Jean and I have lived in twenty homes, four times as many as I lived in growing up.

I still enjoy going back to games at the RAC, where I often run into Joe Boylan on the other side of court doing our radio broadcasts. I see Mark Conlin and his wife, Kathleen, who works in sports marketing at Rutgers. Our teams still keep in touch, and we are able to gather and reminisce at my home in Jersey.

I've finally hung up my Chuck Taylors. I don't have the same lift on my jump shot, and that's how I know I've officially retired from basketball. When I first moved to Xerox headquarters in Rochester in 1988, I played in a men's executive basketball league, and continued until I was in my mid-forties. I'd play against the chairman of Bausch & Lomb. We used to play Monday nights. I loved basketball, but I realized that as you get older, your body doesn't always do what your mind wants. And I saw guys starting to tear their ACLs, so I started focusing more on playing golf.

Dick Lloyd transcended time. He played basketball until he was seventy. He still plays pickleball.

There is no better game than basketball. I always got a lot of enjoyment from playing it.

As I've mentioned, one of the many things that basketball has taught me is the value of teammates. And I realized long ago that my best teammate ever is my wife. When we discussed my taking a job as a project manager at Xerox headquarters in Rochester in 1988, we both knew that if I did not take it, my career would soon hit a glass ceiling. Jean never missed a beat. Our house has always been our home. It has always been well-decorated, warm, and welcoming. This is a gift she shares with our daughter, Stacey, as she is raising her own family.

Many of my positions at Xerox required me to travel a great deal. I was recognized as a million-mile flyer and traveled all over the country. As my career expanded and my responsibilities grew, I began to travel the globe. I was working in countries like Russia and Japan, places I'd never imagined I'd visit. Jean did a great job managing our house in my absence.

She was our children's rock, as she has always been mine.

She is loving but no pushover. She runs her house with the efficiency of a Tom Young practice. It's one of the reasons our children are the way they are today.

She only once shared frustration about shouldering the responsibilities when I was traveling. And when I became president of the North American Solutions Group, she didn't like going to the grocery store with me, because it usually took twice as long to shop—I would run into so many people in the aisles and talk with them all.

We've always enjoyed the summer. When the kids were young, she would take them to the pool or to Point Pleasant Beach when we had a summer home near the boardwalk. I'd fly down and join them on the weekends. We've always liked being near the water.

Jean would take the children jet skiing and boating. She still enjoys doing that today. She used to be an active golfer but gave it up to focus on Ryan when he started playing in high school. "I needed to be home, and Mike was busy with twelve-hour days at Xerox and traveling," she says. "I just got a new set of clubs, so we'll see. When we're in Florida this winter, I'm going to go out, take some lessons, and play nine holes."

These days, I spend a lot of time on the golf course during the winter. It's important to stay active. Every time I think I'm getting pretty good, I realize the exceptional talents of professional athletes. I quickly realized I wasn't in their league, but hopefully I can get my handicap down to the low teens.

I've already been lapped by one member of our family. It is lot easier to lose when it's to your son. Ryan is a scratch golfer and participated two years in the Golden Bear and the Hooters tour for developing PGA players. Then he worked for Xerox for ten years. Now he works in software sales at OneStream.

Ryan still has great memories of Jean's dad taking him to South River High School to hit golf balls when he was five years old. When we moved to Rochester, Ryan became interested in playing in junior tournaments. I hired Craig Harmon, a teaching pro from Oak Hill Country Club, to work with Ryan. Craig's father, Claude, had won the Masters, and his brother, Butch, had worked with Tigers Woods. I wanted Ryan to get proper training. One summer, Ryan played 147 rounds. I played two.

It all paid off. Ryan became one of the top-ranked high school golfers in New York state. "Dad never pushed me. He never pressured me. He let me make my own decision about school," Ryan says. His last official recruiting visit was to Rutgers. He chose the university over some high-profile golf schools.

Ryan was selected MVP and co-MVP of the golf team for four straight years. The team went from nowhere to finishing second in the Big East. Jean and I used to attend all of Ryan's matches in high school and college. His gallery at Rutgers also included Jose Carballal and his wife, Rosalie, and Jean's father, who also got up at five thirty in the morning to watch Ryan practice.

Ryan qualified for the U.S. Amateur after college, and Stacey caddied for him at Pebble Beach. Those two have always been close since ninth grade. "I used to date Stacey's friends, and she used to date mine," he says. Just last year, Ryan joined up with his former college teammate Kevin Campana to win the eighty-seventh New Jersey State Golf Association Four-Ball championship at Forest Hill Field Club in Bloomfield.

Stacey is the light of my life. I'm amazed at how positive, upbeat, and selfless she is with our family. As a child, she loved gymnastics, but the MacDonald genes led her to the basketball court at Our Lady of Mercy School for Young Women in Rochester. She played with Abby Wambach, a star on the U.S. women's national soccer team. The basketball team was good enough to advance to the New York state regional championship. Stacey could have played in college, but she tore her ACL in a state tournament game, and she hung up her sneakers.

When she went to Rutgers, she was eighteen and ready to experience life. "I guess she thought Mike and I were a little strict," Jean says. "She called and said, 'I can't wait to call home at six o'clock in the morning and tell you I'm just getting in from the night before.' Well, a few years went by and she was calling to say she wanted to come home."

Stacey transferred to Saint John Fisher during her junior year. That was a wonderful place for her. She thrived. She was a good student and is quick to point to the fact that she is the only MacDonald to earn a master of science degree. She got it in human resources at the New School in New York City. She had a great business career with Xerox and ADP. She got married and became a full-time mother. She is an avid reader. She is currently the president of an educational foundation benefiting her children's school.

There are eight years between Ryan and Chris. Stacey always liked being Chris's big sister.

Chris got the best toys because he was the youngest and his siblings were out of the home. He was the first child to drive a new car.

Chris is no different from anyone else in our family. He is a competitor. He played tennis in high school but was more interested in academic class rank. He was a serious student who got straight As at Mendon High and went to NYU for undergrad. Chris approaches life with honesty, passion, and rigor. He liked the idea of going to school in New York City, in the most dynamic and fast-paced environment. He is passionate about traveling the world. It's why he spent a semester studying abroad in Prague and why he is my constant travel companion in adulthood. Like me, Chris is always ready for a last-minute trip around the world.

Chris lives in Boston and is the head of artificial intelligence and analytics at PTC, a software company. He also serves as the chairman of Siloam, a wellness center focused on serving those affected by HIV/AIDS, based in Philadelphia. I often kid him by calling him "Big Data," especially when he is talking about advanced technologies that I certainly don't have a handle on. In reality, I'm impressed by his ability to always be learning and evolving.

When Chris was in second grade, he did a project for which he was asked who his hero was. He immediately chose Bill Gates, later realizing after I returned from a parent-teacher night that everyone else had chosen their mom or dad or sibling. As Chris says, "My dad, not one to take offense, thought it was hysterical and still tells that story today. In reality, my dad is more than a hero. He's my rock, providing steady, no-judgment support and advice to anything life throws at you. He's also my North Star, personally and professionally. And not because he has had great success, but the way he arrived at that success always resonated with me."

I take great pride in the fact that all of our children are hard workers. Even though they never had to worry about student loans, they always had part-time jobs when they were in school. It really helped all of them. Ryan had a job in the meat department at Wegmans. Stacey grasped the nuances of business quickly when she worked at corporate offices at Xerox. Chris had summer internships with American Express and SAP. I like to believe my children were far more prepared than I was when I took my first job at Xerox. They knew how big companies worked before they graduated from college.

Now that Jean and I are back in Jersey for half the year, we are able to be part of our grandchildren's lives.

Ryan and Lauren have three children—Reese, Roree, and Ryten, who are thirteen, eleven, and nine, respectively. Reese is going into eighth grade, likes dancing, and belongs to a dance troupe, which would have pleased my mother. Ryten is an excellent three-sport athlete, and Roree loves to play basketball. Anthony and Stacey have two children, Christian and Cameron, who are eight and six, respectively. Christian is also an exceptional three-sport athlete. He and Ryten are best buddies and play in the same Little League in different age groups. Their teams both won championships. Anthony, who is currently a vice president of sales at Presidio, an IT solutions company, coaches Christian in baseball and coached both boys in flag football. One is the quarterback. The other is a wide receiver. Cameron is just starting out in sports, and Stacey coaches her in tee-ball. She also loves dance and gymnastics.

It seems like Jean and I are at a youth baseball or basketball game every night in the summer. "We probably see our grandkids more than other people do," Jean says. "To me, it's my greatest pleasure to see them growing up."

As a grandfather, I feel fortunate to be able to take the children to watch the Eagles, Phillies, 76ers, Flyers, Rutgers, and Ravens play.

It's gratifying that everyone enjoys family time as much as Jean and I do. We take family vacations every year.

In July 2020, we celebrated my birthday by taking a boat trip with the family to the Statue of Liberty. I had lunch with all my grandkids. They gave me a present—two Cross pens with the inscription "From the Bench to the Board Room." Roree wrote me the nicest handwritten letter I've ever received. It says:

Dear Pop Pop, Happy Birthday. You are the kindest and most generous person I've ever met. I've never met someone who works as hard as you. You and Nam Nam are my favorite people to be around and spend time with. You are an amazing grand pop to us. You make us feel so loved. No other grand pop could ever be better at playing shark with us in the pool, bringing us on such great vacations and trips and making us better in basketball. No

*one could be a better Pop Pop. I'm so lucky that you and Nam Nam
are my grandparents. I hope you have an awesome birthday. You
deserve it.*

And you know what? She's the quietest one. She never says "boo."

Seeing the statue on that beautiful day was great. I had gotten the idea
from the captain we hired. He's a former state trooper. I asked him what
we could we do if we wanted to take a ride on the Fourth of July. He said,
"Mike, forget the fireworks. You're out there with a lot of boats. It's night
and it's dangerous. Just go up and see the statue and take the kids in the
morning." The trip lasted five hours total, two and a half hours each way.
We took the kids swimming on the Manasquan River on the way back.
With all this stuff going on during the pandemic, it was a nice thing to do.

I've never forgotten my roots. Though I can't go back in time, I try to
visit my sister and grade school friends throughout the year. It's important to me. I make time to see how things are going at my high school alma
mater, Bonner. I also say thank you to the Augustinians at Villanova. I still
consider myself a Philadelphia sports fan at heart and am grateful to have
seen Wilt Chamberlain play for the 76ers in the NBA finals and to have
watched Pete Rose play for the Phillies. No one screamed louder when the
Eagles won the 2017 Super Bowl.

Sometimes, I'll just drive around Upper Darby to see the old
neighborhood.

It's humbling to think that I, one of seven children whose parents
never owned a home, achieved the American Dream. I could never have
imagined reaching this level of success when I was sitting on the bench
waiting my turn to enter the game.

Acknowledgments

I would like to thank the following for all of their assistance and support on the book. First my wife, Jean, and my entire family. I also want to thank Dick Weiss and his wife, Joan. Dick has been the ultimate partner for me in writing my first book. The many interviews and meetings with players, coaches, executives, and CEOs were accomplished due to his Hall of Fame professionalism. I would like to thank my son Chris and my friend Edward Ciaschi for their help with the process of writing the book—Chris for his great technical support and Ed for helping with the many interviews that were conducted. I want to express my gratitude to Dick Vitale for writing the forward to the book. I was very lucky that Dick came into my life when I was eighteen years old, and we have been friends ever since. I would like to list everyone who was interviewed:

Childhood friend: Nick Cangi

High school teammate: Ed Stefanski

Rutgers coaches: Dick Lloyd, Dick Vitale, John McFadden, Tom Young, and Steve Pikiell

Rutgers teammates: Phil Sellers and Mark Conlin

V Foundation board members: Harry Rhoades, George Bodenheimer, Nick Valvano, Dereck Whittenburg, and Susan Braun

Xerox retirees: Jose Carballal, Richard Cerrone, Richard Shea, Tom Dolan, Emerson Fullwood, Dave Garnett, Lynn Carter, Frank Edmonds, Mike Brannigan, Valerie Blauvelt, Mike Ianacone, and my boss for ten great years, Anne Mulcahy

Former and current Medifast employees: Jason Groves, Mona Ameli, Brian Kagan, Brian Lloyd, Dom Vietri, Tim Robinson, Jeanne City, Meg and Guy Sheetz, and CEO Dan Chard

OPTAVIA leaders: Wayne Andersen and Dan Bell

Former OPTAVIA board members: Charlie Connolly and Jeff Brown

All of the people I have mentioned have been a vital part of my life. My priorities have always been God, family, and the great passion I have always had for my career. I want to thank my sister Margaret and my brother Bob for their support over the years. I treasure the many memories I have of Brad, Florence, Mary, and Marilyn. I love and miss them all. Thank you to the Suydam family, who treated me like a son, and Herb Carman, who was a humble man and a great friend.

My deepest appreciation for all of my Bonner and Rutgers coaches and teammates for six great years of basketball, my great teammates at Xerox and Medifast who helped me along the way, and Jimmy V for creating a foundation that means the world to me.

—Michael MacDonald

I would like to thank the following people for all their assistance and support in this project. First my wife, Joan, who has coauthored books with me in the past and put up with my ever-changing moods for the three months and helped edit the raw copy; Trish Plunkett and her daughters, Mairead, Ailis, and Aine, for lending her husband and their father to help with this book; Mike MacDonald and his wife, Jean; their children, Ryan, Stacey, and Chris; and grandchildren, Reese, Roree, Ryten, Christian, and Cameron for providing a picture of what a nice family should look like; Dick Vitale, whose tireless work on behalf of the V Foundation raised $7.3 million in a virtual gala to raise money for research in pediatric cancer, and his wife, Lorraine; Jeanine Reynolds, who has been supportive of every project I have been involved with, and her three children, Tim, Andrew, and Matt; Anthony Ziccardi and the folks at Post Hill Press; Howie Schwab, the ultimate sports encyclopedia; Hall of Fame basketball columnist Bob Ryan and his wife, Elaine; highly talented, prolific author and close friend John Feinstein; Mike Flynn, a visionary in women's basketball who should have been inducted into the Women's Basketball Hall of Fame long ago; Joe and Betty Anne Cassidy; Scott and Suzanne Schenker; Theresa Grentz, the best women's basketball player of her generation, and her husband, Karl; Lea Miller, the driving force behind Battle 4 Atlantis, and her husband, Jim Tooley, who runs USA Basketball; my attorney Rick Troncelliti; Dave Pauley; American commissioner Mike Aresco, who always fights for the underdog; Chuck Sullivan; John Akers, the editor of *Basketball Times*; Rutgers coaches and players Dick Lloyd, Tom Young, Joe Boylan, John McFadden, Steve Pikiell, Mark Conlin, and Phil Sellers; Steve Richardson from the FWAA and Malcolm Moran of the U.S. Basketball Writers Association; Dave Goren of the NSMA, National Sports Media Association; journalism colleagues Dick Jerardi, Roger Rubin, Ray Didinger, Alan Cutler, and Adam Berkowitz; Brian Morrison, Dr. David Raezer, Sam Albano, Jerry McLaughlin, Larry Pearlstein, Mark Whicker and Robyn Norwood, Lesley Visser, John Cirillo, Steve and Patti Hatchell; the late, great Larry Donald, Mike Sheridan, Jay Wright, and Mel Greenberg; John Paquette of the Big East; Steve Kirschner from UNC; Danny Gavitt and David Worlock and all of the folks in the Big 5; four-footed friends Sadie and Bean; and The Guys and the coaches and players in college basketball who have made coverage of the sport so much fun for me over the years.

—*Dick Weiss*

About the Authors

Michael C. MacDonald has served as non-executive chairman of the board of Medifast, a weight-loss products company, since January 2018. Mr. MacDonald previously served as executive chairman of the board from November 2011 until December 2017. He was promoted to chairman and chief executive officer in February 2012.

Prior to this role, Mr. MacDonald was executive vice president of OfficeMax, from August to October 2011, overseeing the Contract Division, a $3.6 billion division of the OfficeMax Company. Mr. MacDonald spent thirty-three years in sales, marketing, and general management at Xerox Corporation prior to joining OfficeMax. Among his most significant roles was leading the turnaround in North America from the years 2000-2004 as President of the North American Solutions Group, a $6.5 billion division of Xerox. In addition, Mr. MacDonald was president of Global Accounts and Marketing from 2004 to 2007, where he led the re-branding of the Xerox Corporation. Mr. MacDonald also has international experience in marketing, sales, and operations with both Xerox and OfficeMax.

Mr. MacDonald also serves on the V Foundation for Cancer Research.

Dick Weiss is a sportswriter and columnist who has covered college football and college and professional basketball for the *Philadelphia Daily News* and the *New York Daily News*. He has received the Curt Gowdy

Award from the Naismith Basketball Hall of Fame and is a member of the national Sportswriters Hall of Fame. He has also co-written several books with Rick Pitino, John Calipari, and Dick Vitale, and authored a tribute book on Duke coach Mike Krzyzewski.